FOR GOD AND COUNTRY

Four Stories of Courageous Military Chaplains

John and Bonnie Riddle

BARBOUR
PUBLISHING

For a complete list of Heroes of the Faith titles, see page 208.

ISBN 1-58660-837-1

All Scripture quotations are taken from the King James Version of the Bible.

Published by Barbour Publishing, Inc., P.O. Box 719, Uhrichsville, OH 44683, www.barbourbooks.com

Cover illustration © Dick Bobnick.

 Member of the
Evangelical Christian
Publishers Association

Printed in the United States of America.
5 4 3 2 1

FOR GOD
AND
COUNTRY

CONTENTS

introduction

Francis Springer

On April 14, 1865, President Abraham Lincoln, his wife, Mary Todd Lincoln, and several guests attended a performance of *Our American Cousin* at Ford's Theater in Washington, D.C. There an actor named John Wilkes Booth burst into the presidential box, pointed a derringer at the back of Lincoln's head, and fired a single shot at point-blank range before anyone had a chance to lay a hand on him. Lincoln died from his wounds the next day.

Within hours of this tragic event, word reached Francis Springer, a friend and former neighbor of the president serving as post chaplain at Fort Smith, Arkansas. At first Springer could not believe the news. "There must be some mistake," he told the messenger. "This cannot be true!" A short time later, the news was confirmed. Springer prayed privately for Lincoln and his family, knowing a terrible task awaited him. As the post chaplain, it would be Springer's duty to hold funeral ceremonies at the base in memory of the slain president. He didn't know how he would manage the task and provide comfort for the soldiers in his care when his own grief was so bitter. Everyone had lost a president; Springer had lost a president and a personal friend.

Springer and Lincoln had liked each other from the time they first met as neighbors in Springfield, Illinois. Springer had always supported Lincoln and his family, and they kept in touch no matter where their lives took them. Now, alone in his study, Springer fell to his knees, praying and weeping at the same time. "Give me strength, Lord," he begged. "I have work to do for You and must keep myself focused. There will be time to mourn later."

Francis Springer spent nearly a day writing his eulogy. He wanted it to be perfect for his friend, truly a speech from the heart. He trusted God to guide his pen. God answered his prayer, because Francis Springer's eulogy would be considered a fitting tribute to President Abraham Lincoln.

He closed the eulogy with these words:

To American youth, the example of our departed President may safely be commended. Mr. Lincoln was not "descended from a long line of illustrious ancestors," but he ascended from the low condition of a frontier log cabin boy to preeminent honor among the wise and good. From poor and obscure but virtuous parentage have arisen our Benjamin Franklin, our Andrew Jackson, our Henry Clay, and last, but not least, our noble Abraham Lincoln. Youth of my country, be studious, prayerful, and persistent in the pursuit and attainment of a cultivated humanity. Let not your humble condition depress you, but only quicken your energy to rise above it, assured that:

> When the battle is fought, and the victory won,
> Life's trials are ended, and life's duties are done;
> That Jesus your Savior will welcome you home
> To mansions on high where
> Abraham's gone!

Edward McKendree Bounds

There has perhaps been no greater single Christian influence on the subject of prayer than E. M. Bounds. Bounds lived a life of trying times and difficult circumstances, yet he always placed his trust and faith in the Lord. Through years of difficult losses and the struggle of the Civil War, Bounds developed a true depth in his personal prayer life and set out to encourage others in their own.

Publishing first in newspapers and then in books, Bounds wrote of a deep, personal relationship with God. His books pointed to the effectiveness of prayer for the changing of hearts and situations, doing so in a way that touched his readers' hearts and minds.

Though Bounds passed away in the early 1900s, his books still influence the prayer lives of many Christians today. Bounds's ministry continues today through his written words, and his life is a true testimony to the power of God working in the hearts of ordinary people.

George Fox

Some men live as quiet heroes, serving the Lord faithfully in their daily lives. Others are called to display their heroism in a great act that cements their place in history forever. George Fox lived his life in the quiet heroism of service to the Lord until one fateful evening when he was called to live out his heroism in a final act of sacrifice.

At the time, Fox was serving as chaplain to approximately nine hundred men aboard the *USAT Dorchester*. He lived with them, served with them, and ministered to them. Then, just nine hours from their destination, the ship came under attack and quickly began to sink. Men scrambled, some in panic and others too numb with shock to realize what was happening. Fox did not panic. He spent his remaining time on deck helping men into life jackets and lifeboats. His own turn never came.

Fox gave his life jacket to a man who did not have one. His sacrifice was the only option available to him at the time. Three other chaplains were aboard that night; all of them made the same sacrifice.

Surviving men later reported that as they rowed the lifeboats away from the sinking transport, they could hear a song echoing across the cold, dismal sea. The four chaplains could be seen huddled together as they faced the final minutes of their lives. Their shouts of praise and hymns could be heard dancing through the night air—their final gift to those they had served so faithfully.

Robert Preston Taylor

Some human experiences test a person so fully that they either break him or refine him into a whole new level of faithfulness. That is the kind of experience that Chaplain Robert Preston Taylor went through during his years in Japanese war camps, aboard transport ships called "hell ships," and in the midst of the torture and inhumanity that was the Bataan Death March. He suffered torture and mistreatment regularly; watched others die, knowing he was helpless except to pray; and attempted to hold onto the hope that he would one day see his family again.

Taylor not only knew true compassion and servanthood intellectually, he lived them. He spent his imprisoned years in servanthood to those who needed the Lord so desperately and a guide to those who could no longer find a way. He suffered alongside the men in the Bataan Death March, always making an effort to help and encourage them. His trials brought forth a refined life that was used powerfully by the Lord, and he set forth an incredible example of love while living in the love the Lord brought to him.

FRANCIS SPRINGER

one

F rancis Springer was born in the small town of Roxbury, Pennsylvania, on March 19, 1810. German immigrants, his parents were very poor, although his father, John, worked hard as a miner to provide for his family, leaving for his job early every morning and returning home at suppertime. Francis Springer learned the value of hard work as a child; its lessons would stay with him for the rest of his life.

Francis had an older sister, Elizabeth, who had been named after their mother, a woman of strong faith. Although she had to spend much of her day cooking, cleaning, and tending livestock, Francis's mother still found time to love and nurture her children. Life was not always easy for the Springer family, but their love for each other provided a good foundation for hope and optimism.

Life was fairly routine for the Springer family until the War of 1812 broke out and Francis's father traded his pick and shovel for a musket, enlisting as a soldier in the army under the command of General Andrew Jackson. A few days later John Springer said good-bye to his family, not knowing when or if he would see them again. Springer fought bravely against the British invasion and wrote home about many of the battles he survived, including several in which he nearly lost his life.

In 1814, Francis and Elizabeth's mother passed away. Their father, having lived through so many battle-field skirmishes, lost his life the following year, leaving Francis an orphan at the age of five. Before his death, John Springer had contacted several neighbors and friends and asked them to take care of his children if something happened to him. Although he wanted his children to stay together, that was not possible. Elizabeth and the family that took her in stayed in Pennsylvania, but Francis soon found himself living with James Schoaff and his family in Maryland. Schoaff, who operated a small inn, promised John Springer that he would look after his son and care for him until he was twenty-one.

Francis Springer was fortunate to have such a loving family to care for him. Many war orphans were treated horribly by those who adopted them for the labor they could provide, but James Schoaff and his wife, Marie, treated Springer as though he were one of their own children. Because Schoaff was a generous man, he sent the growing Francis to school for six months out of the year. In return, Francis worked at the inn, doing whatever jobs he was asked to handle. It wasn't the same as living with his real parents, but he spent the next ten years of his life with the Schoaffs, generally happy and content.

At the age of fifteen, Springer ran away and eventually found himself in Hagerstown, Pennsylvania. It wasn't that he was being mistreated at home. He was not really sure what he wanted to do, but he was determined to find a way to earn his own living and do something positive with his life. He had ambition, and there wasn't far to go in Hagerstown. He was fortunate to find a job as a furniture-maker's apprentice and worked hard at learning the trade. He put in long hours to learn everything he could about making fine furniture and eventually specialized in ornamental sign painting. Francis Springer was proud of his new-found trade, sure that he had finally found his place in the world.

As happy as he was, Springer still felt as if something were missing from his life. He began attending church services, hoping to find the answers he needed there, and was surprised by how much he enjoyed his weekly church visits. He began looking forward to hearing the preacher talk about the Word of God at Sunday services. His heart was opening to God's Word, and before long, Francis Springer started receiving religious instruction from a pastor of the local Lutheran church.

The pastor, Benjamin Kurtz, soon realized how much his star pupil was dedicated to the Lord. He encouraged young Springer to work hard, study the Bible, and always walk a straight and narrow path. "My son, always remember that God loves you and has a plan for your life," Reverend Kurtz told Springer on many occasions. In his teens, the young man became an influential member of his church. Despite his youth, Francis Springer realized that the Lord was speaking to him and took comfort in knowing that God had a plan for his life.

two

At the age of nineteen, Francis Springer began thinking about a career in ministry. "Nothing would give me more pleasure than spreading the Word of God to people who need to hear the message," he said to his pastor. "I want to serve where I am needed by the Lord, but I need to get a good education first." In 1829 he enrolled in classes at Pennsylvania State College at Gettysburg, where he quickly discovered the difficulties of Latin. His tutor, David Jacobs, was fair but very strict. He made sure that Springer learned the language properly. Springer had no trouble with any other course, but Latin seemed to be impossible to master. Through a combination of prayer, hard work, and study, he finally became fluent in Latin, impressing the instructors with his accomplishment.

Four years after entering Pennsylvania State College,

Francis Springer graduated, electing to continue his studies for three years at the Hartwick Seminary in New York State. Upon graduation from the seminary in October 1836, he was licensed as a minister in October 1836 by the Lutheran Synod of Maryland. The following year he was ordained.

Springer's first assignment in Maryland was exciting and challenging. Because he was a new minister, he was bound to be assigned to a small congregation. He found himself serving poor families near Clear Spring in Washington County. He traveled among several churches in the area, preaching sermons and teaching school whenever an opportunity presented itself. Although he did not earn a lot of money, he was happy in his ministry. A few months later, Springer met a woman named Mary Kreigh, who was from a large family in the area. Their backgrounds were as different as night and day. He was an orphan who barely remembered the family he was born into, and she was the only girl in a family of nine children.

After a brief courtship, Francis and Mary were married in the spring of 1837. Two years later they moved to Springfield, Illinois, where he began looking for preaching opportunities. He was devoted to the church and felt an obligation to continue working in ministry. Because of his love of teaching, he opened the doors to his home and established a small school for local children. At the same time, he began holding church services in his parlor and attracted many people who were interested in learning more about Lutheran services and the Word of God.

Francis and Mary were enjoying their new roles in the community. Before long, Springer found himself in charge of a trade school for boys—the Springfield Mechanics Union. Francis could not believe how fortunate he was. Life was finally coming together for him. He was married to a woman whom he loved more than life itself and was actively working in ministry and serving the Lord.

In 1844 a new family moved next door to the Springers. Abraham and Mary Todd Lincoln and Francis and Mary Springer began a friendship that would last for years to come. Lincoln and Springer came from similar backgrounds and had a lot in common. Born into poverty only thirteen months apart, both men worked hard to get an education and become successful in their professions. By 1850 Francis Springer had made a name for himself as a minister and educator; Abraham Lincoln was a prominent attorney and politician. Both men disliked slavery and loved poetry. They were also interested in mechanics and science. Lincoln went on to become the only United States president to hold a patent.

Francis Springer continued to enjoy life in Springfield, but early in 1847 he received a formal invitation to serve as the pastor of St. Paul's Lutheran Church in Hillsboro, Illinois. He did not hesitate for a second and accepted the new position with a passion. He was still committed to serving the Lord and felt good about his new responsibilities. Because he was now in a high-ranking position in the Evangelical Lutheran Synod of the West, he was soon called upon to create a Lutheran college in his community.

There was already a school in the community— The Hillsboro Academy—but it was having financial problems. After much prayer and careful planning, Francis Springer approached the academy and asked if he could take over the school. Within days, he was the chief administrator of the newly named Literary and Theological Institute of the Lutheran Church of the Far West.

In addition to his duties at the school, Springer continued preaching and serving where he was needed. Because he was an ambitious man who liked to keep busy, he also started editing the *Prairie Mirror*, the local weekly newspaper. He enjoyed his duties as the editor, which would lay the foundation for his future experience as a correspondent for several newspapers during the Civil War.

By 1852, Francis Springer returned to Springfield, Illinois. He brought his family with him and relocated the Literary and Theological Institute of the Lutheran Church to Springfield. Soon the name of the school was changed to Illinois State University. The college had plenty of resources to offer its faculty and students, including a large library of fifteen hundred books, a science lab, and a vast collection of natural history specimens.

Soon the board purchased land and erected the college's first building, made of expensive stone and brick.

For the next several years, Springer continued to operate as the president of Illinois State University, but in 1855 he resigned to pursue a new interest in politics. He felt compelled to help his old friend Abraham Lincoln, who had become the new spokesperson for the Republican Party. Springer had been following the political career of his former neighbor and supported him through all his endeavors.

When Lincoln ran for Senate in 1858 and lost, Francis Springer was there to encourage and minister to him. Lincoln continued to wage his campaign against slavery and won the presidential election in 1860. In February 1861, when Lincoln left Springfield for Washington, Francis Springer sent him the following note:

> *I cannot repress my desire to say to you, good-bye! I did not call in person, for this purpose, because I know you were pressed with enough company.*
>
> *When the train bearing you passed my residence this morning, my heart said, God bless Lincoln, & make him second to none but Washington!*
>
> *Be assured (I speak what I know)—that thousands of earnest prayers daily ascend to Heaven for you & our beloved country.*
>
> *Yours with very great respect,*
> *Francis Springer*

Springer continued to correspond with President Lincoln and wrote articles for several newspapers encouraging the country to rally behind its new leader. The work he did so selflessly for his friend, putting aside his own aims and goals, did not lead to fame for Springer but was necessary and worthwhile, or he never would have done it.

three

Francis Springer and his family were enjoying life in their comfortable home in the country. They had eight children, and it was evident that they were a happy family. In a time when fathers were often stern and reserved with their children, Springer enjoyed playing with his on the large lawn. They did, after all, have nearly enough children for a good game of baseball.

In 1861, Francis Springer was serving as the superintendent of public schools in Springfield, Illinois. By now, he had plenty of experience as both an educator and a pastor, and the lessons he had learned in both careers helped him become a strong family man of faith. He enjoyed the challenges that came with the superintendent's job and looked forward to helping the students succeed in their studies.

Although he was basically an administrator, he took time out of his busy schedule to meet personally with many of the teachers on a regular basis. They saw him as a positive role model for both themselves and their students. Springer never abandoned his work with the church. He was still fervent about working in the ministry and continued to preach every Sunday. He had a passion for working with the poor, an interest that grew out of his own roots.

After Confederate forces opened fire on Fort Sumter in April 1861, the vast majority of northern religious bodies ardently supported the Union. When the Civil War began, Francis Springer was a fifty-one-year-old pastor and educator, a loving husband, and the father of eight children. He was not happy to see the country so seriously split and so many young lives put in danger, but like most people at the start of wars, both he and his wife believed the war would be over soon. Their friend Abraham Lincoln would see to that, with God's help.

Husband and wife had many conversations about the war and the impact it was having on the country. An early victory had not come as predicted.

"The fighting is throwing a blanket of sadness over all of the families who have lost loved ones," Springer said. "It must end soon, before another soldier has to lay down his life for his beliefs."

Despite their daily prayers asking God to end the war as quickly as possible, the fighting seemed to intensify instead of going away.

A call for volunteers found Francis Springer and his seventeen-year-old son, John, enlisting together in the Tenth Illinois Cavalry. Springer explained his enlistment to Mary: "I love you, Mary, but I feel the Lord is calling me to serve our country. I will write to you every day and do my best to come home safely and quickly." Because of his age and pastoral experience, Springer was given an officer's commission and appointed a chaplain. When he received his orders, he felt a sense of peace, certain that God was guiding him and placing him where he was needed the most.

Springer quickly adapted to his new duties as a chaplain. He enjoyed holding weekly church services and ministering to the men in his unit. He was a very personable man, and everyone he served seemed to find comfort in knowing they had such a dedicated chaplain. As chaplain, Francis Springer was dedicated to leading his fellow soldiers to Christ and to being there to fill every one of their spiritual needs.

When he began serving as a military chaplain, Springer kept a record of his daily life in the army. He recorded not only the activities and events that took place, but also letters he sent home to his wife and children. Because of his experience working at several newspapers, Springer began writing occasional columns for newspapers that were eagerly awaiting any type of news from the front lines. In his journal, he also recorded copies of every newspaper article that he penned while serving in the Civil War. His journal was eventually published as a book titled *The Preacher's Tale,* which was edited by William Furry and published by the University of Arkansas Press in 2001.

four

Francis Springer was sure that he was exactly where God wanted him. Serving as a chaplain allowed him to use his gifts of mercy and faith, something that many of the soldiers had never witnessed before. In addition to holding Sunday church services, Springer encouraged the men to write home and helped those who could not read or write very well, if at all.

The soldiers who wore the blue and the gray shared many similarities. Most had been farmers before the war. They jumped into the conflict as volunteers in 1861 with the belief that the war would last only a few short months. Others volunteered later or were drafted into service, convinced they were needed but afraid for their homes, farms, and families while they were away.

Though politics and causes were different, Yank and Reb alike served to protect their homes, their states, and the rights each soldier deeply believed to be just. Most of the soldiers were young men; their average age was approximately twenty-one. Within a few months of service, many of these young men were hardened veterans of severe battles, experienced in the rigors of the march and the horrors of war. For most, wartime service was a brutal journey into manhood.

The life of a soldier in the Civil War was an arduous one. It meant many months away from home and loved ones, long hours of drill, a tent for a home, and many days spent marching on hot, dusty roads, burdened with everything a man needed to be a soldier as well as personal baggage to make his life as comfortable as possible. Long stretches of boredom in camp were interspersed with moments of sheer terror on the battlefield. To the thousands of young Americans who left home to fight for their cause, it was an experience none of them would ever forget.

Every soldier wore a wool uniform, a belt set that included a cartridge box, cap box, bayonet, and scabbard. A haversack carried his rations, a canteen, and a blanket roll or knapsack that contained a wool blanket, a shelter half, and perhaps a rubber blanket or poncho. Inside was a change of socks, writing paper, stamps and envelopes, ink and pen, razor, toothbrush, comb, and other personal items. Most soldiers learned to travel light, discarding items that were of no use in the field.

Francis Springer's life in the field was no different from that of other soldiers. He had to carry his own equipment and supplies, and he risked his life every time a battle or skirmish broke out. Before long, he realized that his duties as chaplain were needed in the area of morale. For these civilians turned soldiers, getting used to the rigors and demands of army life was difficult. Most of them had been farmers for many years, never having experienced a need to obey orders. Discipline was a difficult concept to understand, especially when the officer one had to salute may have been the hometown postmaster only a few weeks before. The uniforms were not quite as fancy as those worn by the hometown militias, and soldiering did not always mean fighting.

There were fatigue duties such as gathering wood for cook fires. Metal fittings had to be polished, horses groomed and watered. Fields had to be cleared for parades and drill, and there were always water details for the cookhouse. Guard duty meant long hours pacing up and down a well-trod path, day or night, rain or shine, always on watch for a foe who might be lurking anywhere in the hostile countryside. A furlough was hard to come by. Every man was needed in the field, and few had a chance to visit home.

"Home" in the field was a rectangular piece of canvas buttoned to another to form a small two-man tent, or "dog tent" as the soldiers called them, because only a dog could crawl under one of those tents and stay dry. Every Union soldier was issued one tent. The tent could be pitched for the evening by tying each end to a rifle stuck in the ground by its bayonet or stringing it up to fence rails.

Confederates did not receive shelter tents, though some were issued a variation that they pitched as a lean-to or shelter. As the war progressed, it was very common for a Confederate camp to be filled with captured Union tents, captured blankets, canteens, and haversacks. Confederates especially prized the Union rubber blankets, which were unavailable in the south.

Each man had to learn the marching drill, company and battalion drills, and pay attention to commands given in the field. The infantryman learned the Manual of Arms for the rifle-musket. Most were drilled in it so well that they could recite the steps in loading and priming for years to come. The soldiers drilled as squads and in company formations. After an hour of drill on that level, the regiment took to the field for regimental level drills and parades. Drill and military procedures were a part of the daily routine that every man eventually grew accustomed to.

For the infantry, drums and bugles were used to announce daily activities from sunrise to sunset. Reveille was sounded to begin the day, followed by an assembly for morning roll call and breakfast call. Sick call was sounded soon after breakfast, followed by assemblies for guard duty, drill, or to begin the march. Francis Springer would often visit the men who lined up for sick call, because many of them were in need of spiritual guidance as well as medicine. Drummers were also important to keep the soldiers in step during parades and call them to attention. In battle, drums were sometimes used to signal maneuvers and give signals for the ranks to load and fire their weapons. Springer quickly learned all the signals and assisted some of the younger soldiers who were having difficulty understanding them.

The artillery and cavalry relied solely on buglers, who were as important in their roles as the drummers were to the infantry. When not playing for their respective regiments, the musicians were combined with regimental or brigade bands to play marching tunes or provide field music for parades, inspections, and reviews.

The armies camped out until the arrival of the winter months, when they would establish winter camps. Log huts large enough to accommodate several men were constructed with mud-chinked walls and a roof made from tents or sawn boards. Most had wood bunks built inside as well as a small fireplace for warmth. These lasted only a few months and then it was back to the field and shelter in the smaller tents. Francis Springer, like most of the other soldiers, found some comfort in those winter camps.

Leisure activities were similar for both officers and enlisted men, and much of that time was spent in writing letters home. Soldiers were prolific letter writers.

Springer helped any soldier who needed assistance in writing letters due to illness or battlefield injury. It was the only way for them to communicate with loved ones and inform them of their condition and where they were. Springer kept his promise to his wife and wrote to her every day. He would share the experiences and trials that he had to endure and talk about the successes that he had in ministering to the troops. He also wrote notes to his children telling them to listen to their mother and promising that he would be home as soon as he could.

The arrival of mail in camp was a cause for celebration no matter where the soldiers were, and much grumbling occurred when the mail arrived late. The lucky soldiers who received letters from home often read and reread them many times. Packages from home contained baked goods, new socks or shirts, underwear, soap, towels, combs, and toothbrushes—all items that were expensive to purchase in the field.

Free time was also spent in card games, pitching horseshoes, or team sports such as the fledgling game of baseball, which rapidly gained favor among Northern troops. Soldiers also played a form of football that often resulted in broken noses and fractured limbs. Holidays were celebrated in camp with feasts, foot races, horse racing, music, boxing matches, and other contests. Many soldiers kept pets including cats, squirrels, raccoons, and other wildlife. Francis Springer provided an opportunity for weekly Bible studies and lessons about Christ for anyone who was interested. While at first very few soldiers attended, after a few battles and a little time away from home, attendance increased.

The Union soldier received a variety of edibles. The food issue, or ration, was usually meant to last three days while on active campaign and was based on the general staples of meat and bread. Meat usually came in the form of salted pork or, on rare occasions, fresh beef. Rations of pork or beef were boiled, broiled, or fried over open campfires. Army bread was a flour biscuit called hardtack. Called "tooth-dullers," "worm castles," and "sheet iron crackers" by the soldiers, hardtack could be eaten plain, though most men preferred to toast it over a fire, crumble it into soups, or crumble and fry it with their pork and bacon fat in a dish called "skillygalee." Other food items included rice, peas, beans, dried fruit, potatoes, molasses, vinegar, and salt. Baked beans were a northern favorite when the time could be taken to soak them and a cooking pot with a lid could be obtained. Coffee was a most desirable staple. Some soldiers considered the issue of coffee and accompanying sugar more important than anything else. The coffee beans were given out green and unroasted; it was up to the soldiers to roast and grind them. Like most of the soldiers in his unit, Francis Springer had no choice but to adapt to this new way of eating. He wrote home and asked that baked goods and other treats be mailed as often as possible.

The soldiers loved to sing, and there were many favorite tunes that were popular in both armies. A variety of instruments were available to musically minded soldiers, including guitars, banjos, flutes, and harmonicas. More industrious soldiers fashioned string instruments such as fiddles out of wooden cigar boxes. Springer used this opportunity to introduce several hymns that many of the men had not heard in the past. Before long, they were asking Springer to teach them more hymns.

Discipline in the military was very strict. The provost marshal of the army was responsible for enforcing military rules, but regimental commanders were given the authority to dole out punishments for minor offenses. Francis Springer and the other military chaplains serving in the Civil War were instrumental in helping the soldiers adjust to taking orders. Petty offenses such as shirking camp duty or not keeping equipment in good order were usually treated with extra duties such as digging latrines, chopping wood, or standing extra hours on guard duty.

Insubordination, thievery, cowardice, or other offenses were more serious, and the guilty party was usually subjected to embarrassing punishments such as carrying a log, standing on a barrel, or wearing a placard announcing his crime.

five

After months of training and preparation, Francis Springer's regiment was assigned to Cane Hill, Arkansas. It was a long and difficult journey, because they did not depart until November 13. After many cold and rainy days and nights, the soldiers and their chaplain finally arrived at their destination on Saturday night, December 6, 1862.

Along the way several of the soldiers became ill. Francis Springer tried his best to meet their spiritual needs when they made camp at night.

He would ask them if they were Christians, and he remembered one young man's reply. "I have been, but I have gone astray, sir," said an eighteen-year-old boy who was suffering from a high fever and flu-like symptoms. "I am afraid that Christ has forgotten about me, because I have not been living the life of a good

Christian," the young soldier said to Springer.

Francis Springer gently laid his hand upon the young man's shoulder. "Christ still loves you, no matter what you have been doing with your life." He told the boy to pray and ask Christ to forgive him, promising that he would immediately receive the forgiveness of the Lord.

The young man immediately asked God's forgiveness, and Springer could see the sadness lift from his face. Even though he was still sick, he told Springer that he was feeling better inside. "Thank you, sir. Thank you for being here for me."

Springer would pray for the soldiers in his unit every day. He prayed that Christ would look after them and protect them and that they would find a sense of peace and comfort in knowing Christ loved them. During battle, he would pray for the soldiers on both sides.

The soldiers in the unit were exhausted by the time they reached Cane Hill, having traveled an average of thirty miles a day over rough terrain in all types of weather. Even the horses appeared to be in need of a rest. Everyone finally got a good night's sleep.

Francis Springer and two other officers, including one of the surgeons, sought shelter in the sparse but dry and comfortable home of an old missionary named Reverend Trot. Trot welcomed the officers with open arms, made them a hearty meal, and gave them a place to sleep. Everyone felt welcomed by the man's hospitality and enjoyed a good night's sleep out of their tents, the cold rain, and wind.

On Sunday morning, the men found themselves scurrying to prepare for an attack by the Confederate army. Several scouts had galloped into camp with bad news: A large regiment of Confederate soldiers was camped in the adjacent hills. The general in charge consulted with his officers, and everyone agreed that the enemy was indeed within striking distance.

As the men prepared to break camp and advance on their enemy, another scout reported that a nearby house had recently been deserted. "It would make the perfect place for a field hospital," he reported to his superior officers. They agreed, and within a few hours Francis Springer found himself assisting the surgeons and nurses as they set up their equipment and supplies in the makeshift medical unit.

Before long the surgeons and nurses had established a field operating hospital in accordance with army regulations. Fresh linens and bedding were in ample supply, and fires were burning in all the fireplaces. Everyone was ready to handle casualties from the battle, but Francis Springer would have preferred that the hospital not have any patients pass through its doors that day, and he relayed his wish to God.

God must have been listening, because they only had time to treat one young soldier who had been wounded in the leg before the order came to evacuate the hospital. The surgeons and nurses quickly treated the soldier, who was in severe pain and bleeding from a bullet that was still buried deep inside his leg. There was just enough time to remove the bullet, bandage the wound, and send the young soldier away in an ambulance. As quickly as they had worked to establish the field hospital, everyone chipped in to tear it down and evacuate to a safer place. The word quickly spread among the regiment: A large battle would take place within the hour.

Their regiment quickly assembled and marched toward the Confederate unit. A few miles later, Francis Springer found himself praying for a swift end to the imminent battle, with minimum casualties for both sides. "Dear Lord, please keep us safe, no matter what color uniform we are wearing," he would pray. He found himself praying this prayer on many occasions during his service in the Civil War.

The battle took place in an area known as Rhea's Mill, which was a little over seven miles from their original campsite. Fortunately, only a few shots were fired and no injuries were reported. The opposing army was nothing more than a band of scouts, no doubt eager to fire a few shots and return to report what they had discovered. But Francis Springer quickly learned that this was not the real battle, and a few of the officers tried to prepare him for the worst. "We won't know what we are going up against until we get there," one officer told him.

A scout had been able to get close enough to the Confederates to get a good estimate of their firepower.

Once the young soldier made his report to the general in command of Springer's unit, plans were made to move to Prairie Grove, about six miles away from Rhea's Mill. Within minutes Springer could feel the excitement and apprehension in the air. He continued to pray for everyone, including the enemy. He knew of the horrors that lay ahead and asked God to have mercy on everyone that day.

Within an hour the regiment was in place, ready for battle. Seasoned and new soldiers alike stood ready to defend their position and carry out their orders. The sun was shining brightly when the first shots were fired, but within minutes Springer was deep in "the fog of war." Hell on earth unfolded before his eyes, sometimes in slow motion, other times too rapidly to be understood. The nonstop sound of muskets being fired, along with cannon and artillery fire, was deafening. In a few minutes soldiers on both sides were wounded and killed. The sounds of the screaming wounded filled the air. Springer risked his life by staying on the battlefield and assisting the surgeons and nurses who tried to treat the wounded as quickly as possible. He prayed for those who had already died and for the wounded in so much agony. Springer knew that the Lord had sent him on this perilous journey to minister to these soldiers, and he was not going to let the sound of muskets firing around him keep him from doing his job.

He later wrote in his journal:

> *Sublimity and grandeur of mortal combat are*
> *qualities of war I do not care to appreciate. I will*
> *not so train my heart that my moral nature shall be*
> *perverted to a taste for carnage. War is an aveng-*
> *ing hell that grows naturally and inevitably from*
> *the fruitful sail of brutish human passions. For war*
> *makers, Jesus has no blessing; but for peacemakers,*
> *they shall be children of God.*

Springer's first battle continued for several hours before the Confederates pulled back in defeat. Hundreds of soldiers from both armies lay dead, their bodies strewn across the battlefield in unlikely, unnatural poses. Some of the soldiers who survived the initial fighting died over the next few days from their wounds.

Francis Springer spent many sleepless nights assisting the surgeons and nurses wherever they needed his help. He also prayed with all the wounded soldiers and tried to offer them comfort. Springer would never be the same man that he was before the first shots of his first battle had been fired. Although he still felt God's calling to serve in this ministry, his heart ached for the men who had died and those still suffering from near-fatal wounds.

Over the next few days, their regiment saw no additional fighting, which left plenty of time for Francis Springer to catch up on his duties as a chaplain. Whenever possible, he would hold prayer sessions. On Sundays, he tried his best to hold services. After the first battle, more soldiers were interested in learning how to pray and wanted to hear more about Christ's love and mercy. Springer was eager to oblige and felt good about his ministry of spreading the Gospel.

The next several weeks found the regiment on the move, tracking units of the Confederate army. After only a few weeks of life on the battlefield, he was ready to go home—as was every other soldier in the conflict—but his job was not finished. As long as they were under orders to continue into battle, he would do his duty.

He watched the young boys who made up the majority of the regiment become hardened to the rigors of daily life in the field. Their regiment was becoming better at tracking the enemy, and Springer saw fewer casualties on the battlefield. His own prayer time increased, allowing him to spend more and more time with the Lord, praying for a swift end to the war.

A few weeks into the new year, Francis Springer was temporarily assigned to the provost's office in Fayetteville, Arkansas. While he was grateful to be out of harm's way, he was concerned for the men he had to leave behind. He was also grateful to be working and sleeping in dry quarters, a feeling that ashamed him to some extent but was totally natural.

In Fayetteville, Springer and others he met there spent their days administering the oath of allegiance to citizens who came out to join the Union army. From 9:00 A.M. until 4:00 P.M., a seemingly endless line of people showed up to enlist. Every one of them was eager to join the battle to defend the Constitution and laws of the United States. Although he was not supposed to pray with each person who enlisted, Francis Springer did so openly and with a passion. He encouraged each new recruit to pray with him and was able to bring a few souls to Christ while working in Arkansas.

Before long, Springer found himself back on the battlefield. His regiment had been ordered to chase and attack a unit of Confederates that had been spotted nearby. Anxiety and adrenaline ran high because the soldiers did not know what to expect. They had faith in the scouts that were running ahead of them, but they also knew that the scouts could be killed, leaving the regiment to walk straight into an ambush.

A few hours later the shooting and mayhem began. The Confederates were spotted camping at the base of a small hill. Though they had the element of surprise on their side, several dozen Union soldiers were wounded and killed. Throughout the battle Francis Springer assisted the surgeon and nurses as they tried to treat the wounded and remove the dead. He found himself praying nonstop and often wondered how much more he could endure, but he never lost faith in God and knew that he would never abandon the ministry that had been placed in front of him.

After nearly an hour of fighting, the Confederate soldiers retreated to safer ground. Exhausted, hungry, and cold, the regiment quickly regrouped and set up a camp. Once the campsite and perimeter had been established and secured, the soldiers not on duty were allowed a few hours of rest. There was no rest for Francis Springer, who had several dozen severely wounded soldiers to attend to.

One young soldier had been wounded beyond hope. The surgeon tried his best to save his life, but there was nothing more that could be done. The boy was within hours of death and aware of his condition.

"Reverend, will you pray for me?" the young soldier asked Springer.

"My son, I will pray for you now and will pray for your family back home."

That seemed to give the dying soldier some peace and comfort. The young soldier confessed that he had been a believing Christian when he was younger but had stopped attending church services. "Will Christ still love me?" he asked the chaplain.

Springer assured him that indeed Christ did still love him. "He has not abandoned you, my son," he told the dying soldier. "Christ only asks that you ask Him into your heart, and He will remain with you throughout eternity."

That seemed to give the boy a sense of assurance, and with Springer's encouragement, he said these words right before he died: "Here, Lord, I give myself to Thee!" After assisting with the burial of the body, Springer collapsed into his tent for some much-needed rest.

In early March, Francis Springer found himself

en route from Fayetteville, Arkansas, to Springfield, Missouri. The journey took exactly one week, and he traveled with several other officers who, like himself, had received orders to report to Springfield to officiate at a funeral. Nearly two dozen men made up the delegation. Along the way they met up with a government-sponsored wagon train of about sixty wagons, but it was traveling too slow for them, so they continued on without escort.

A Christian woman by the name of Mrs. M.S. Tilson, a widow from Lake City, Minnesota, had been working as a matron in one of the hospitals at the Springfield post ever since the death of her husband. She gave of herself tirelessly and ministered to the sick and wounded soldiers. Although she was only forty-three, she died of typhoid pneumonia. The army was very grateful for her service, and as a tribute to her had arranged a special funeral.

At the funeral Francis Springer read several scriptures and gave a short eulogy as a tribute to the fine woman who had been loved by many people, military and civilian alike. Springer described the funeral in his journal:

> *The scene was novel and impressive. Several companies of the 18th Iowa and one company of the 13th Kansas, all under command of Major Campbell of the former regiment, formed the military escort, headed by a full band of drums*

*and fifes. It was truly grateful to generous minds
and likewise touching to witness the burial of a
lady attaché of the army, who had ventured far
from her kindred and home, to share the doubtful
fortunes of the campaign in order that she might
alleviate the sorrows and sufferings of the brave
men gone forth to battle for their country.*

While visiting Springfield, Missouri, Francis
Springer had the opportunity to meet a Reverend
Jones, who had worked as a missionary in the Indian
Territory for nearly forty-two years. They prayed
together and shared stories about their adventures.

A few weeks later Springer received some very
good news: He was allowed to travel home to Springfield, Illinois, for a leave of absence. The journey took
him several weeks, and he experienced much of the
inconvenience that was the norm for traveling such a
long way in those days. At times the weather was so
rainy he thought he might catch pneumonia and die
along the way. The roads were rough and muddy,
but at least he did not suffer any enemy attacks, and
finally he arrived safe and sound on April 17, 1863.

He was met by his wife and children and many of
his friends as he rode into town. Everyone wanted to
celebrate his safe return and did not even want to
think about him going back to the battlefields. During
the next several weeks, Francis Springer became reac-
quainted with his family. He also preached at several

churches where the people were eager to hear of his adventures.

Springer told about the horrors of the battlefield and how difficult it was to witness so many lives being lost and injured. He told of the joys of bringing new souls to Christ and how he was pleased to be serving God as a chaplain in the army. He asked everyone to pray daily for a swift end to the fighting. "Too many lives have been lost, and I fear that many more will die in the weeks and months to come," he told them.

Francis Springer enjoyed several months of leave before he had to return to active duty in early July. He kissed his wife and children and shook hands and hugged all his friends who had come out to see him off. He had orders to report to Springfield, Missouri, and he would be traveling with another officer, a Lt. Col. E. J. Searl. He later wrote about that day in his journal:

> *I hurried from the scene with satchel in hand. My face was once more toward the army and my back toward the loved ones at home—my wife, daughter, and sons. May God protect, guard and save them!*

Along the way Springer and Searl encountered many people who had been forced to move from town to town in search of family members, a way to make a living, or a little bit of hope and peace. Springer and

Searl were delayed in St. Louis because of a paperwork snafu. Apparently the military officials had not sent along the proper paperwork for the two men to travel with the several hundred pounds of supplies they were bringing with them.

After successfully obtaining the proper authorization, the two men continued on their long and arduous journey. When they arrived in the town of Rolla, Missouri, Searl went ahead to Springfield while Springer waited several days before a seat was available on a stagecoach.

Springer had to stay at a hotel called the Amos House, which was filled with profane and rude people. The town itself mostly consisted of saloons, billiard halls, tin-pan alleys, and several shooting galleries. Although he attempted to pray for the town's residents, he was met with resistance. He longed to return to his unit and minister to his men.

A local preacher invited Springer to hold church services, and he accepted the offer, preaching to a small congregation of soldiers and local citizens who assembled in the courthouse. Another chaplain—Reverend Caves—who was the chaplain of the Twenty-third Missouri Infantry Volunteers, attended church that day, and Springer asked if he would close the service with a prayer. Despite the cold, dirty courthouse, Springer found some peace that day.

After a three-day layover in Rolla, Springer continued on his journey. He stopped along the way in

Cassville, Missouri, and preached to the soldiers of the First Arkansas Infantry. Springer was very encouraged by the large attendance and later in the day held a Bible study for the soldiers.

While in Cassville, he was joined by his unit, which had been ordered to hold fast there for a few weeks. Violence and vandalism were running rampant in town, and it was thought that a military presence might have a calming effect on the rowdy townspeople. The longer the war went on, the more violence seemed to thrive among the civilian population. He prayed for calm to come over the town and urged everyone to attend Sunday church services.

Over the next several weeks Springer witnessed large groups of refugees coming into town. A few came by horse and wagon, but most walked. All of them were hungry and carried only a few possessions, but the common factor that drew them all together was their poor spirits. They had been through so much trauma that they just did not care anymore. Now Springer knew exactly why God had stationed him in this place. His new ministry would include citizens of all ages and backgrounds, people who needed to be healed spiritually and emotionally.

Springer immediately started holding prayer services all over town. When the need arose, he also ventured out of town to see people who were camped nearby. Slowly the people started to trust him and Springer felt as if he were making some good progress.

One day as Springer was walking through town, he saw a man hiding in some nearby trees. He appeared to be dirty and disoriented, so Springer quickly went over to try and help him. Before Springer could reach him, the mysterious man slipped into the woods that surrounded the town.

Over the next several days Springer kept an eye out for the man, who would come a little closer to him each time he made an appearance. He would bring food and water and place it in a basket near the trees. The weather was getting colder, so he also included a blanket and a clean shirt, socks, underwear, and pants. He was not sure of the man's size but thought he could come pretty close. Springer believed the man must have experienced a horrific trauma, perhaps in the throes of battle. He had seen symptoms of war-related stress over the past few months, and it saddened him to see people suffering that way. He prayed an extra prayer for that man and for everyone else the war was affecting.

Springer's prayers were answered a few days later when he was finally able to talk with the man. His assumption had been correct: The man had witnessed his entire family being killed by Confederate soldiers. He broke down and cried in Springer's arms for what seemed like an hour. Springer prayed for the man and for his deceased family. The man attended church services later that day but left when it was over. Springer never saw him again but never forgot that man and what he represented. "This war is lasting too long," he said to his fellow officers. "Too many innocent lives are being torn apart."

A few days later the regiment received orders to head toward Bentonville, in Benton County, Arkansas. They made the march of twenty-five miles in one day, traveling in the hottest part of August. They passed several houses and farms along the way that had either been abandoned or burned down, no doubt by rebels or bands of thieves who were roaming the countryside. By the time they set up camp, everyone, including the horses and mules, was exhausted and hungry. Springer offered to hold a prayer service, but no one was interested in attending; everyone was anxious to get a good night's sleep.

The next day they suddenly found themselves breaking camp and marching with new orders. This time they were called on to escort a wagon train of nearly one hundred wagons. The road was hot and dusty, and they kept having to stop and make repairs on wagon wheels that were damaged by the rocks and holes that littered the way. During the breaks, Springer was able to hold short prayer services for military and civilians alike.

A few days later Springer and his regiment received orders to break away from the wagon train. They left a few soldiers with the civilians as protection, hoping that would be enough. In addition to Confederate soldiers, wagon trains were often attacked by bands of thieves and various Indian tribes. There were reports that Indians had taken over Fort Smith in Arkansas, in conjunction with several units of Confederate soldiers.

Finally, after traveling nearly four hundred miles, Springer's regiment arrived at its destination, Fort Smith. They set up a temporary camp and waited for the scouts to return. No campfires were allowed; the element of surprise was a priority for the officers. Springer could feel the anticipation of the upcoming battle. Men were restless, trying to keep busy without thinking about what lay ahead. Springer used this opportunity to hold a small prayer meeting and was surprised by how many people attended. "Prayer will help keep you closer to Christ," he told the soldiers. "Remember to pray for yourselves and for your enemy."

The scouts returned to report that Fort Smith seemed to be deserted. The general in command felt that they needed to break camp immediately and charge the fort. Springer thought about his wife and his children back home at that moment, and ached to know if they were okay. He said an extra prayer for his family and charged toward Fort Smith.

The general had been correct in his decision to charge the fort. What little enemy force had remained there quickly escaped into the nearby woods. Fort Smith was now occupied by Springer's regiment. The soldiers were quick to adapt to their new surroundings and took comfort in sleeping under a roof once again.

The tide seemed to be turning, and Springer could feel the tension disappear from the troops. The anxiety and apprehension that had been felt only a few hours before was gone.

Fort Smith was actually a combination military post and civilian town. Many of the civilians had been hiding and were delighted to witness the arrival of nearly four thousand Union soldiers. It appeared that things were taking a turn for the better, but that feeling was short-lived, and over the next several weeks and months a build-up of enemy troops near Fort Smith continued.

For some reason, communication with their military leaders had been cut off. Never before had Francis Springer felt so isolated and alone, a feeling that was quickly spreading throughout the fort and town. Rumors were running wild about how Confederate soldiers would come charging into the fort, or how Indians were going to sneak in under the cover of night and kill everyone in their sleep. Springer did his very best to stop the rumors from circulating, reminding everyone to trust in the Lord. "He will never abandon you," he promised.

The Lord had not forgotten the troops and civilians of Fort Smith. They suffered several long months of isolation, but no enemy attacked the fort. In early November, the majority of the forces in the regiment left the safety of the fort to attack the Confederate army that had been building up nearby. They were greatly outnumbered, so Springer prayed that somehow the enemy would retreat before any shots were fired. Much to the surprise of the officers in charge, the Confederate army, over seven thousand troops strong, ran off and refused to do battle with the Union soldiers. Springer thanked God for a miracle that day.

six

Francis Springer served faithfully as a military chaplain for six years, but when he returned home, he was happy to put the war behind him. He was not bitter, but stronger, because he had served not only his military leaders but Christ as well. Christ had called him to go and minister to soldiers and civilians alike, and Springer had answered that call. He had endured many hardships and risked his own life on many occasions as he prayed and cared for the spiritual needs of everyone he encountered.

Francis Springer was a generous, compassionate, obedient servant of the Lord who had reached out to thousands of people during his six years of military service as a chaplain. It was an experience that he knew he would never forget, no matter how old or feeble-minded he might become.

After the war was over, Springer created several charitable institutions to aid the orphans of the war. One, in Springfield, Illinois, was called the Home for the Friendless. Today it goes by the name of the Family Service Center. The other was the Fort Smith Orphans Asylum, which is no longer in operation. Through those two institutions he was able to help thousands of children who otherwise would not have had a place to live. Before long both institutions were successfully placing orphans with families who wanted children.

In addition to his work with charitable institutions, Francis Springer continued to preach at his home church and officiated at weddings and funerals.

He received high honors when the Illinois Adjutant General's Office issued its report on the history of the Tenth Illinois Cavalry, the unit Springer had served with. They wrote in a report that:

> *The regiment was fortunate in having for its chaplain Reverend Francis Springer, who was among one of the most efficient chaplains of the armies; preaching to the command whenever an opportunity afforded; at all times visiting and looking after the comfort of the wounded, sick and dying soldiers. Doctor Springer is remembered with kindest regards and esteem by all.*

Francis Springer spent his remaining years in

Springfield, Illinois, with his wife, children, family, and friends. Mary Springer, his wife of forty-five years, passed away in 1884. Francis Springer lived for another eight years, dying at his home on October 21, 1892.

EDWARD McKENDREE BOUNDS

one

From a young age, Edward McKendree Bounds, better known as E. M. Bounds, was blessed with a loving family that would forever influence his life and the paths he would choose to take. Born in 1835, Edward was the fifth of six children, having two older brothers, two older sisters, and a younger sister. The Bounds family was strong in its faith and sense of family. They had a profound impact on their town, even when Edward was still a child.

Thomas Jefferson Bounds, Edward's father, was a man of faith and action. In March 1836, when Edward was just nine months old, Thomas mapped out and organized the town of Shelbyville, Missouri. Purchasing land at auction, Thomas and his family settled in the town and set out to build a new life there.

The town of Shelbyville, Missouri, was strongly

influenced through the Christians who settled there. Although the first official church was not opened until 1840, the nearly four years between the founding of the town and the building of the church were fruitful for the Lord. During that time Thomas was influential in forming the first Temperance Society in Missouri. The campaign was very successful, reaching not only their own town, but the entire county.

Edward was blessed to not only see the large movements and campaigns as a youngster in Shelbyville, but also the day-to-day ministry that went on. Even before an official church was founded, there were regular prayer meetings, Bible studies, and area preaching days. "It is always important to follow God and meet together with God's people," Thomas Bounds would explain, encouraging young Edward to enjoy fellowship in the Lord.

Out of those early meetings a camp meeting was developed, with the assistance of pastors from other counties. God worked mightily through the camp meetings, using the pastors to speak to the hearts of the people. The response was tremendous, and desire grew for a church in which to worship and gain spiritual guidance.

In 1839 a Methodist Bible class was founded, and in the spring of 1840 the First Methodist Church of Shelbyville was built. The church stood on a knoll overlooking the town, beckoning the people. Edward McKendree Bounds attended and was influenced by the ministries of the town's church and Christian Fellowship.

Thomas was a natural-born leader with the keen ability to think through situations. He was often called on to help make decisions in town matters. He served in numerous political arenas, serving as both the clerk of the county and the clerk of the court. A financially prosperous man, he was involved in the building and running of the town's hotel, Smith City Hotel. He also built a mill to supply flour to the town's growing population.

Perhaps one of Thomas's greatest accomplishments was his influence in the formation of the County Agricultural Society when he was selected to draft the society's constitution. His draft became a model for agricultural societies throughout Missouri, Kansas, and Iowa.

Edward had a deep respect for his father and the work that he had committed his life to. That respect would influence his own life as Edward sought to follow his father's footsteps and influence the lives of others.

The year 1849 turned out to be a difficult, troubling time for the teenaged Edward. He had found a second friend and mentor in his eldest sister's husband, Rev. William Vandeventer. "Uncle William" was Edward's encourager, playing a special role in the young man's life. William would sit for hours and discuss the Bible with young Edward, always letting him know the importance of God's Word. "Edward, you are God's workmanship, and you can have the honor of sharing this good news with others," he would say.

After many years of joyful influence in Edward's life, William became ill in the spring of 1849. After seven months of battling the flu-like illness, William was taken home to the Lord. Edward was hit hard by this loss, having to deal with his own pain while trying to help his sister grieve the loss of her husband.

During an already heart-wrenching time for the family, Thomas Jefferson Bounds came down with tuberculosis. On September 13, 1849, at the age of forty-four, Thomas was taken home to be with his Lord and buried in the city cemetery. Thomas's absence was mourned throughout the city and county where his influence and provision were remembered.

Although the losses of both William and his father were difficult for Edward, they did send him on a spiritual journey that would lead him to a life of great influence.

Edward began to take a more active role in family decision making and leadership. His oldest brother, Thomas, inherited the responsibility of the estate left by their father. Edward assumed household responsibilities, and his opinion was well respected in financial matters.

Shortly after the losses suffered by the family, John Bird, Edward's cousin, began discussing the possibility of gold mining in California. Charles, Edward's other brother, began to consider mining as an option. When John and his family decided to join a caravan heading west, Charles decided that he would join as well.

A close bond had formed between Charles and Edward when they were young boys, and they often sought out adventures together. This time was to be no different. Charles set out a plan that would take them both west, although Edward was only fourteen and Charles sixteen. Edward agreed to join the trip, which was sure to be an adventure and perhaps the chance of a lifetime. How could he possibly not go? He was young, and easy wealth lay to the west for young men not afraid of hard work.

With their eldest brother, Thomas, remaining to oversee their father's investments, Edward and Charles were free to pursue their dream. Preparing quickly, they left with the caravan and their family's blessings and prayers. They spent a rough winter in Nebraska with distant family members, but as soon as the way was passable in the spring, they continued their journey.

The brothers made their way to a California canyon called Mesquite. The desolate canyon was not what the young men were expecting, but their enthusiasm remained as they ventured into the mining camp of Placerville in Eldorado County. The camp would hold many surprises for the young men.

Work at the mining camps was difficult and tiring. Days were often long, stretching out before them with no promise of success. Although they labored hard at their task, the boys soon discovered that the difficult work and the rough lifestyle of the mines were not what they wanted to do with their lives. Seeking to live out their faith in God for as long as they remained at the mines, the brothers were faced with many troubling situations along the way.

Perhaps one of the most troubling issues for Edward was how to use his free time at the mining camp. Most men passed their free time in saloons and gambling halls. Edward and Charles watched men let their hard-earned money slip away at such places, confident that their "big strike" was just around the corner. Never having been exposed to such a style of living, Edward quickly discovered that he had no use for it.

Edward had watched his father gain stature and financial security through hard work and faith in the Lord. Vowing to follow God and not fall into the painful and sinful trap of chasing money, Edward and Charles set out to live their lives for God in the midst of the camp.

Remaining at the camp for four years, the brothers worked hard. They spent long days in labor and sought much-needed rest when their day was done. By the end of the four years, both decided that although they had learned valuable lessons from their time at the mines, it was not where they wanted to live. The brothers left the mines together, heading back toward their family in hopes of pursuing whatever path the Lord would lay before them. Although they left without earning the huge financial gain of which they had originally dreamed, they had gained spiritual awareness of immeasurable value.

two

Arriving back in Missouri, the brothers settled in St. Louis for a time, to make plans for their futures. Inspired by the mighty barges that traveled up and down the Mississippi River, Charles began a freight business that became a profitable success. Edward took some time to help Charles begin his business while trying to decide exactly what he wanted to pursue himself.

In the spring of 1854 Edward decided to attend law school. Since he had been a small boy, Edward had found great enjoyment in hearing about his father's political endeavors. The decision to enter law school came as no surprise to his family. They were all aware of Edward's keen intellect and his fascination with the political workings of the up-and-coming country. Leaving St. Louis, Edward ventured to Hannibal to begin his studies.

Edward was a quick study. He had always had a sharp mind and a willingness to work hard to achieve his goals. He moved quickly through his studies, taking delight in all he was learning as he pressed toward his goal. At the young age of nineteen, Edward completed his studies, becoming the youngest lawyer in the state.

Edward set up his law practice in Hannibal for the next three years. He was moved with concern not only for his own spiritual condition but also that of those around him. Keeping in touch with many family members and friends, he began to hear of great revivals throughout the nation.

In the late 1850s America went through a series of changes and transitions. It was a time of preparation for the coming Civil War and the strife that would accompany it, threatening to tear the young nation apart. One of the most noticeable acts of preparation for such trials was a great season of revival.

Springing forth on the East Coast like a well of living water, the revivals spread rapidly across the nation. Termed the Great Spiritual Awakening of 1857–58, the waters of revival swept people up and drew them into relationships with God as they committed their lives to Him. Edward began hearing more and more stories of God working in awe-inspiring ways throughout the nation and was profoundly affected himself when he attended a revival meeting along the banks of the Mississippi River.

Evangelist Smith Thomas had traveled up and down the Mississippi, spreading God's Word. In early fall he arrived in LaGrange, a small port city just north of Hannibal, seeking to spread God's Word and inspire the people to seek after God with their whole hearts.

Edward had been hearing about such meetings for some time. Having the opportunity to attend one himself, he prepared to make the short trip to hear Smith Thomas speak. Edward arrived at the revival meetings as a lawyer with a heart for God; he would leave the meetings with an entirely new direction for his life. Having felt the stirrings of a greater call for quite some time, Edward committed his life once again into God's hands, expressing his desire to live for God with his whole heart.

In opening himself to God's hand on his life, Edward quickly realized that he had been hearing God's call and his time as a lawyer was coming to an end. Knowing that he was called to ministry, Edward sought God's Word and prayed continually for the guidance he would need to once again change the course of his life. He found the courage and strength he needed through God's power, returning to Hannibal to conclude his business dealings as quickly as possible.

Once free from his remaining responsibilities in Hannibal, Edward moved to Palmyra, Missouri, to begin his formal education in ministry. He attended the Centenary Seminary of the First Methodist

Episcopal Church South, spending two years in prayer and learning as he grew in his spiritual walk. After graduation his official ministries began and his life took on a whole new shape.

three

By the time Edward was completing his second year of training, he had already gained a reputation as a true servant for the Lord. Due largely to his family's legacy and his own personal achievements, Edward's accomplishments were quickly noted. He rose to the top of his class and became a noted speaker in his region. Edward threw himself into the Word, learning concepts that would lead to ideals and convictions that he would share with others.

Having a deep-rooted faith—both in his own heart and through the influence of the godly examples who had surrounded his life—Bounds found a passionate conviction for the truth of God's Word. His years as a lawyer had taught him many things that would be useful to him in the ministry. One was a firm grasp on the art of public speaking. Bounds had no problem slipping into the role of public speaker. He learned how to understand God's Word in his own heart and impress that wisdom on the hearts of those to whom he spoke.

The thrill of receiving his first official ministry assignment was topped only by the fact that the letter of recognition was signed by Rev. Cornelius Vandeventer, his late brother-in-law's father. The letter of recognition was not easy to come by, though; first he would have to preach in front of the pastors of the Methodist community.

February 21, 1860, was an exciting day in the life of E. M. Bounds, the day he would attend the Hannibal Quarterly Conference and preach to the gathering of pastors, who would then decide on his future in the ministry. Bounds had developed a passionate, bold style of preaching, combining deep spiritual truths with powerfully moving words. He could stir even the hardest of hearts.

On that day he stirred the hearts of the elders and pastors, who made a unanimous decision to recommend Bounds to the Methodist Episcopal Church South.

Edward M. Bounds,
   God has called you to the ministry and is working powerfully through your life. Go, and serve the Lord with all of your heart, mind, and soul.

He received the letter of recognition held so dear to his heart and officially ventured out into full-time ministry.

Even in his earliest days of ministry, Bounds was full of enthusiasm and zeal, stirring his flock on toward a deeper love for God. Traveling the often cold and rough road from town to town and farm to farm, Bounds found that he had a great deal of time to spend with the Lord, developing his passion for prayer and seeking God's purpose in his words.

As he traveled his circuit, Bounds hosted prayer meetings and Bible studies as well as full days of preaching. His words were often stern, yet they were full of compassion, compelling listeners' hearts as he spoke and taught from the Word. His circuit grew, and more people came to know the Lord.

Earning his living however it was provided to him, Bounds was incredibly grateful for the support that his flock provided. The hardworking farm families found ways to support Bounds by sharing parts of their harvest and opening their homes to the man who opened God's Word for them.

Through that first year of ministry, Bounds's organizational skills came strongly into play. God worked through him to not only teach the people, but to lay a strong foundation for the Bible schools that would soon be built. Bounds's strong belief in the discipline of education—both in the Word of God and the practical applications of literature, math, and science—compelled him to lay the groundwork for future schools and found a seminary.

Bounds began what started out as a small Bible academy but quickly grew into a seminary. Not only was ministry taught there, but all other educational needs were addressed as well. Students were taught through the convictions of Bounds's heart, stressing the disciplines necessary for achieving goals and working hard, while at the same time serving as an inspiring example to show them the way. The school went on to become very influential in the region, training and equipping many for the tasks that God would lay before them.

Bounds's first year of ministry was packed full of inspiring events that stirred his heart and refreshed his soul. He might have continued on in this same vein of ministry for many years to come, were it not for the shots fired at Fort Sumter on April 12, 1861.

four

The Bounds family believed strongly in justice and equality, seeking to love others as God loved them. In that vein, Edward's father had "rented" a young slave girl and her mother, so they would not be sold off and separated. They were welcomed into the Bounds household and treated with all the care and respect of a family member. There was concern that this might be viewed as condoning the practice of slavery, but the family looked to the mother and daughter's needs and sought to do right by them in God's eyes.

Slavery was not an issue to Edward. He had grown up with the young "slave" girl in the household and saw that she was not somehow less of a person. He had always held to the belief that the merchandising of people for any purpose was morally wrong and against God's teachings, be it in the slavery of the South or the sweatshops of the North. Bounds was deeply disturbed by such treatment of people, and could not support it in any way.

The Civil War was not fought strictly on the issue of slavery, as some have come to believe. Many opinions and debates went into the issue, particularly in the state of Missouri, which was faced with a series of crises that turned the focus from slavery and onto the unfair treatment of all people by those in power in the North. It was a very tricky issue, with wrongs on both sides, leaving Bounds in a difficult position as war approached and decisions had to be made.

Bounds wrestled with the issue of who was right, the Union or the Confederacy, but he was not able to come to a clear conclusion. He saw a war being fought not about slavery, but about greed and manipulation. Both sides were fighting for their industry and the money it would make them, and both sides were breaking laws along the way. Having studied the Constitution in law school, Bounds knew that legally a state had the right to choose to leave the Union. He felt that the Union was not justified in keeping the states from separating, should they so choose.

He also saw the Confederacy fighting on the basis of greed, supporting the concept of slavery and refusing to yield to discussions and compromises. With both sides having valid arguments, Bounds found the approaching war corrupt on all sides. There were no easy answers, and though he sought God's hand in the situation, he was not clear on how God would want him to speak about the issues.

At first Bounds decided to remain completely out of the debate. He was, after all, no longer in the political arena; he had a busy life shepherding his flock and spreading God's Word. As it turned out, events to come and the leadership of the State of Missouri would draw him into the midst of war and forever change his life.

During this turbulent and trying time, Edward's brother Charles met a woman and fell in love. Bounds traveled to the wedding, which took place on April 23, 1861. He enjoyed the company of his family and friends as they celebrated his brother's marriage, knowing the relaxation would not last long. The coming trouble hung heavily on everyone's mind and was often the talk of the event.

A short while later, on May 10, 1861, the St. Louis massacre occurred and Missouri found itself in the middle of the conflict. The state guard, technically neutral but actually Confederate sympathizers, were guarding the arsenal at St. Louis. On May 10, General Lyons marched his Union troops into the city, outnumbering the state guard by nearly seven thousand men. Lyons claimed the arsenal for the Union. The guards were forced to surrender and were taken prisoner.

The disturbance had drawn quite a bit of attention, and as the new prisoners were marched away from their post and down the streets of St. Louis, a large crowd began to gather and taunt the Union troops. The troops responded by firing their weapons into the crowd, killing twenty-eight people as the event grew out of hand. Most who died were civilians; some were children.

This event spurred on Missouri's anger and its support for the Confederacy. In the crowd that fateful day were two witnesses who would later play a pivotal role in the course of the war, William T. Sherman and Ulysses S. Grant. Word spread quickly, and although the state government attempted to remain officially neutral, the tide had turned toward the Confederacy. General Lyons blamed the event on the unruly crowd that had taunted the Union troops, but he was considered a murderer by the people of Missouri, and their outrage would not be easily removed.

In the months following this tragic event, Bounds watched many of his fellow laborers sign on as chaplains. During these confusing months Bounds was surprised to receive a new assignment. He would be leaving his current area to take over a church in Brunswick, Missouri.

Arriving at his new location in late October, Bounds found that war consumed the conversation and thoughts of the residents, much as it did throughout the nation. Brunswick was the hometown of a number of Confederate soldiers. It was only a few miles from where a battle was fought in Lexington, so there were strong opinions on what was happening.

Bounds was once again torn, not sure what was right in God's eyes.

Bounds continued to preach submission to authorities, since he firmly believed that God's Word called for such action. He struggled, though, when he saw the authorities in Missouri misusing their power and causing harm to innocent citizens.

Bounds was called to preach at the funeral of a seventeen-year-old boy who had been accused by the Union of being a "bushwhacker." Without trial or evidence, the soldiers took the young man to the Grand River and held him under the ice until he drowned. Bounds preached at that funeral, having known the young man and fully believing his death was not justified.

Bounds continued to preach God's Word and minister to the people. In June 1862, he wrote his quarterly conference report, letting his superiors know that his church was averaging seventy people and growing in many ways. Though war and its consequences weighed heavily on the hearts of the people, Bounds knew God had a greater purpose, and he sought to lead others to the Lord, even in the midst of the turmoil.

five

In September 1862, Missouri was placed under martial law, infuriating the citizens and creating havoc among them. Union provost marshals were given complete authority within the state, allowing them to do as they pleased without accounting for their actions. This caused the people of Missouri to embrace the southern cause even more closely, and the events that soon followed in Palmyra in many ways cemented the fury at the power the Union soldiers then held.

In early October, while marching through the city of Palmyra, Confederate General Joe Porter saw an opportunity to gain arms and create problems for a small garrison of Union forces. While the Union forces occupied the courthouse, Porter began firing down on them from the Methodist church. A battle ensued that further divided the people of Missouri and the Union.

The battle enraged Provost Marshal Stracham, often referred to as "the Beast," who had already vowed vengeance against Confederate sympathizers. On October 18, 1862, he selected ten men falsely accused of being General Joe Porter's troops. They were given an immediate sentence of execution by public hanging. One young wife pleaded with "the Beast" for her husband's life. After she met his ungodly demands, he ordered her to choose someone else to die in her husband's place. Unable to sentence another innocent man in her husband's place, she did not know what to do.

A young man with no wife or children realized what was transpiring and offered his life in the exchange. His only request was that his mother be informed of the events and it be made known to her that he died honorably. Bounds, the young man's pastor, was once again called upon to preach at a funeral that should have been avoided. It was later revealed that none of the men had anything to do with General Porter or his troops.

Because of martial law, Stracham had the ultimate authority, and the incident received almost no official recognition. The only official inquiry occurred several years later, when falsified documents were found attempting to justify the killing of the ten men.

The culmination of all these events, particularly the hangings in Palmyra, caused Bounds to wonder if and when civil disobedience was acceptable. Was there ever a time when the people were justified in going against their governing party? How was he to combine what he knew was right by God's Word with what he was seeing happen around him? The overall cause of the Union may have been just, but the actions taking place in Missouri were far from justified and caused more and more people to turn from the Union in favor of the Confederacy.

Amid all these questions and conflicting ideals, Bounds was faced with the need to make the ultimate decision as to where his allegiance lay. A list was compiled of 250 men who were to be taken into custody and offered the chance to pledge their oath to the Union. In addition to their pledge, they would also need to pay a ransom of five hundred dollars to gain their release. The individual men were on the list for a multitude of different reasons, but all were accused of having Confederate sympathies.

Bounds's name was on the list because he was part of the Methodist Episcopal Church South, and any organization with the word South in it was considered suspect. In reality, the word had nothing to do with any political alliance. It was simply a term that had been used to make a distinction between geographic locations. Nevertheless, his name was included, and he had a decision to make.

The ransom money was used by the Union to repair damages done by troops in battle. Railroads and bridges were being destroyed, and the Union needed to fund the repairs. Bounds was against the way citizens were being taken advantage of. Such a sum of money could not be demanded with no legal reason. Even under martial law, such a demand was robbery, not ransom.

"As a citizen of this nation, and a peaceful man of God, this accusation and its consequences are unconstitutional and are not of the Lord." Bounds spoke out against the list and the injustice of what was happening to him and the others.

Bounds had neither the money nor the inward conviction to pay the bond, much less pledge an oath to the Union when he was already an American citizen. As a result he found himself arrested along with 249 others. The treatment of the men was in many ways deplorable. They were shipped out on the open cargo deck of a steamship in the midst of winter, with no extra clothing. Arriving at their destination in Jefferson City, the prisoners were then placed in the stockade until their numbers became too great. They were once again shipped off, this time to St. Louis. Upon arrival in St. Louis, they were taken to a makeshift prison that was a medical center confiscated from a Southern sympathizer.

The conditions of the prison were terrible. The cells were too small and too crowded for the prisoners to lie down in, so they leaned against the wall and rested their feet against each other to sleep standing up without falling. Food often came from Union soldiers' leftovers. The prisoners were not given clean plates or utensils and were expected to share what they had during the eating periods.

For the most part the prisoners were not officially arrested or convicted of any crime. They were simply being held on suspicion and the chance that they might be Confederate supporters. Angered and surprised by the Union's treatment of these clergymen simply because they had the word South in the name of their church, Rev. W. G. Eliot wrote a letter to President Lincoln expressing his disgust at the methods the authorities were using under the guise of martial law. In fact, the letter heatedly pointed out, the arrest and holding of people with no evidence was unconstitutional and not even permitted under martial law.

General Curtis, who also received a copy of the letter, was only antagonized by its contents. The general, fueled with anger over the death of his son, turned his attention toward the clergy involved and grew more hostile with every passing day.

During this time of captivity, Bounds did his best to remain focused on the Lord. He is noted for spending much of his time singing and praying, encouraging other prisoners to join in. He sought to uplift those around him, even in such perilous conditions. He had even hoped to hold a Christmas Eve service for the prisoners, but General Curtis would not allow it.

On December 31, 1862, General Curtis enacted Banishment Order 23 which, in conjunction with a second order by Lieutenant F. A. Dick, required Bounds to leave Missouri. He was ordered behind the lines of the Confederacy and was not to return to the Union until all problems and rebellions had ended.

Just three days after Bounds was placed on a ship that would transport him to Tennessee and then to Arkansas, President Lincoln responded to the letter of protest. He reprimanded General Curtis and ordered all mistreatment of the clergymen to cease. It was just a few days too late for Bounds. He was already on a ship and headed for imprisonment behind Confederate lines. Even then, when God's timing seemed to be working out all wrong, Bounds chose to trust.

"There is a purpose in all things," he would say to the other prisoners.

"How can you be so sure?" they would often ask in return.

In those times, Bounds was able to share his faith, and in those opportunities he found that God was using his imprisonment for good.

As Bounds was transported from one southern point to another, he gained strength from the stories of the Apostle Paul. He, too, had been in chains and mistreated, and yet Paul chose to worship God and allow his life to be used for the Lord's glory. Bounds desired that same attitude, and as the ships traveled onward, he set out to be an example for those around him. Beginning ministries for the captives as best as he was able, he praised God and spoke often of what the Lord had done in his life. The other prisoners began to question how such joy and submission was possible in circumstances as dire as theirs were, and so Bounds's ministry aboard the ships began. Speaking of a joy that comes from the heart and a peace that understands God is always in control, Bounds shared the gospel with those around him. Amazed and encouraged by the outwardly frail and yet inwardly strong man, the prisoners began to listen to his words. God used Bounds to change the lives of many of the prisoners.

For awhile it seemed as though the travel would never cease. As soon as Bounds arrived in one place, orders would come to transport the prisoners somewhere else. In the span of a few months Bounds was transported to eight different locations throughout the Tennessee and Arkansas area. Chaos seemed to abound in most areas. Soldiers and citizens attempted to prepare for more attacks while recovering from previous battles. It was a turbulent time for all those involved, and Bounds once again found himself set in motion, shipped off one final time to a prisoner exchange camp in Washington, Arkansas.

Settling into the prisoner exchange camp, Bounds went about his work of sharing the gospel to the fullest of his abilities. Washington, Arkansas, often termed "Missouri in exile," was where many of those who fled Missouri had settled. In and around the camp were many family members and friends of those he had known in Missouri. Bounds felt the camp was a blessing to him, since he was once again able to fellowship and enjoy the company of those he knew.

Bounds was a strange contradiction. He was a small man who appeared frail and worn down by all that he had endured. At the same time, he was a powerful speaker and godly witness who had a great impact on the lives of those in his circuits. Those in charge of the camp were never quite sure what to do with him. Colonel J. E. Glynn was head of the camp, and he was particularly at a loss as to what to do with Bounds. As word of war spread through the camp, Bounds discovered that his old friend General Sterling Price was now fully in the war and fighting on behalf of the Confederacy. Bounds wanted to join his friend and continue to spread the gospel to the war-torn soldiers of the South.

On February 20, 1863, Colonel Glynn released Bounds from bondage and gave him a pass through the lines of war to the Southern states, where he would be able to meet up with General Price. Though he was no longer a prisoner, Bounds was still held to the banishment order that kept him from returning to any Northern state. The hardships of imprisonment behind him, Bounds forged onward, discovering a new round of treacherous challenges ahead.

Once out of the prisoner exchange camp, Bounds set out on foot. He covered rough ground and forged his way through picket lines and battlegrounds as he headed east toward Tupelo, Mississippi, where

General Price was believed to be stationed. Having walked over two hundred miles, Bounds, weak and struggling to continue, arrived in a small town called Pine Bluff. He needed to stop and rest. Bounds was able to make a deal with a Methodist farmer who allowed him to stay on and recuperate for a few days. When it was time for Bounds to be on his way, he agreed to pay the farmer two hundred dollars for a mule. The farmer waived payment until after the war, should Bounds survive.

Bounds, now traveling with help of the mule, made his way southeast, crossing over into Mississippi in his quest for General Price. He was greeted with the news that General Price was on the other side of the Mississippi. Leaving the mule, Bounds gained passage on the Great Northern for his next leg of travel. Soon the train was turned around and rerouted in order to take supplies to troops in Jackson. Not wanting to go backward, Bounds got off the train in Abbeville and walked to Camp Pritchard. The camp was southeast of Holly Springs and was the location for many Missouri troops. General Price was located quite a distance away.

Having arrived at the camp once again worn from his journey and foiled in his attempts to find General Price, Bounds decided he had a choice to make. He might never find General Price in the trek across the war-ridden countryside. To keep trying could hinder what he could be doing for the war effort. Bounds decided not to search out General Price. On February 7, 1863, at the age of twenty-eight, Bounds joined the Confederate army in Camp Pritchard, Mississippi. He was pleased to be assigned to the Missouri Third Infantry Company B, commanded by General Bowen.

six

As the months passed, Bounds found that the life of a military chaplain was stressful, often painful work. The battles raged on, taking the lives of many soldiers and leaving others with broken bodies and grieving hearts. Bounds would not be deterred in his mission of sharing the gospel, and he sought to be a shining light in the dark times of war.

Word spread of a revival stirring up the troops. The soldiers' hearts were open, and they were experiencing a strong revival of their faith and a new commitment to their Lord. This time of growth lifted the spirits of the weary chaplains and reminded them that God was truly at work in their midst.

Father John B. Bannon had a deep impact on Bounds's life. Father Bannon, known as the "fighting Catholic chaplain," was deeply committed to Christ and ministry on the battlefield. While most chaplains remained at the back lines, Father Bannon served on the front lines where men in serious condition needed his spiritual guidance. Bounds saw how Father Bannon gave every effort for the soldiers he served and drew strength to do the same in his own ministry.

"Edward," Father Bannon explained, "men will respect you when you meet them where they are. Just as Jesus came to heal the sick, we are called to attend to those who are in the most dire need. That will often be the men on the front lines."

"Aren't you afraid on the front lines?" Bounds asked.

"There is nothing to fear when we trust in the Lord. In life and in death, I choose to trust in God."

On March 10, 1863, marching orders were received: The men were to move to the city of Vicksburg. As they progressed toward Vicksburg, they marched through the small town of Linden. Hearing of the hardships the soldiers had endured and wanting to ease their burden if only for a time, the people of Linden opened their homes to the men. Many of the weary soldiers accepted the generosity and enjoyed the rest and a home-cooked meal. That night a large crowd gathered at the town church to hear E. M. Bounds speak about the saving grace of the Lord. With singing and prayer the people came together to worship the Lord, and many came to a saving knowledge of Jesus Christ.

General Martin E. Green was deeply moved by the service and the message that Bounds shared. Among much rejoicing, that very night General Green committed his heart to the Lord.

Two days later, after official camps had been set up, Bounds received his new orders. He would be transferred to a portion of the troops under General Green, the First Sharp Shooters of the Arkansas Volunteers.

Arriving at his new location, Bounds was delighted to find that two of his cousins were stationed in that very camp. Able to catch up on news from his extended family, Bounds was refreshed by his cousins' presence and enjoyed the time of fellowship with them. Included in that fellowship was another man with whom Bounds had much in common. Colonel Cockrell was a committed Christian and member of the Methodist Episcopal Church South. Like Bounds, he had also practiced law in Missouri. The men found that they shared many of the same experiences and quickly became close friends.

Although he had been around many battles by the time spring came, Bounds had yet to experience being in the midst of a full-fledged battle. He would not have to wait long. On April 29, Grant started a series of attacks targeting the troops who fortified the eastern shore of the Mississippi. These attacks included the Fort of Grand Gulf, where Bounds and his men were stationed.

As the battle intensified, the Arkansas Sharp Shooters were deployed to combat sniper fire from the ships. In a tragic afternoon, a round of cannons hit the rifle pit, killing more than eleven men and leaving many more wounded. The Missouri Third was called in for backup, and the battle continued. Bounds, inspired by Father Bannon, refused to go to a safer location. Staying with the troops, Bounds manned the front lines, offering prayers, encouragement, and support to the wounded.

The heat of battle continued for many weeks, leaving the soldiers exhausted and wounded. Through it all, Bounds remained faithfully with his troops. During the day he could be found in the thick of the battlefield, and at night he led worship and prayer services. The services were attended widely by the Confederate soldiers. Sometimes the singing would travel through the silence of the night, crossing enemy lines and inspiring the Union soldiers to sing along. They, too, suffered greatly and sought the comfort of the Lord.

As time passed, new troops were brought to the front lines, and for a time Bounds and the men he served were called back from the battlefield to receive a new assignment. The group was sent to Jackson, Mississippi, on a mission of mercy. There was a desperate need for medical supplies at the army camps, so Bounds's group was sent to bring back what they would need to tend to the wounded.

Bounds spent a night at the Methodist College on his route to Jackson and was pleased to bring back medical supplies, Bibles, tracts, and newspapers. He spent a day in Jackson picking up supplies at the hospital and preparing to leave early the next morning.

Awakened in the night by the sound of gunfire, Bounds soon discovered that the city of Jackson was under siege by General Grant. Bounds was somehow able to gather the supplies and get out of town. He arrived back at his post with the news that Jackson, Mississippi, had fallen to the Union.

The next stop for the Union troops would be Vicksburg, where Bounds was stationed along with many other companies. On May 15, 1863, as Union forces were making their way swiftly to Vicksburg, General Pemberton sent troops to hold off any further advance. Union and Confederate troops met on Champion Plantation. The Missouri troops proved that day how valuable they were to the Confederacy, holding off the troops in a tough and lengthy battle. Impressed with the Missouri men, whose spirit and tenacity others greatly admired, General Pemberton held them in high esteem.

Bounds had remained in the heat of the fighting, and as troops began to withdraw, he was a constant and comforting presence for the wounded.

It became increasingly clear that the city of Vicksburg would not be able to hold off the Union soldiers for very much longer. General Pemberton ordered the Missouri troops to reinforce weakening areas of defense. The order allowed Bounds much more freedom of movement, and his ministry extended as the Lord moved in the hearts of the people.

Bounds saw that his mission to bring light to the city was being carried out. Men were attending the prayer meetings and worship services in greater numbers every day, and Bounds was overwhelmed with the amount of support he received for the town of Vicksburg itself.

As the city of Vicksburg came closer and closer to defeat, other chaplains began to flee.

"There is no need to remain. There is nothing more we can do," the other chaplains claimed as they packed their things.

"It is our duty to stay with our troops. We can be their spiritual guide in these troubling days," Bounds countered, drawing on the wisdom he had gained from Father Bannon.

Chaplains preparing to leave knew the city would succumb to Grant and wanted to be out of the way when that happened. Bounds could not support such a decision, feeling it was his duty to stand by the troops and townspeople, offering them the spiritual support such a time would require.

On May 19, 1863, the official siege of Vicksburg began. The city was torn apart by gunfire and cannon fire. In the midst of the fighting, Bounds was sworn in as a captain in the army. It was a rare honor for a chaplain to receive such a rank, but Bounds had stayed with the troops, and they awarded him with the rank as a way of protecting him should he be captured. Having the rank would entitle him to better treatment and military courtesy in the event that Vicksburg was taken by the Union.

The battle for Vicksburg progressed for weeks. Bounds was deeply affected by the constant gunfire and battling that went on around him. He had to learn to trust God in an even greater way and turned to the Lord in prayer for himself, the soldiers, and the divided and struggling nation. As the weeks slipped into months, suffering, hunger, and death became everyday struggles for the soldiers and the people of the city. Adequate supplies could no longer be received, and at times the fighting became so severe that civilians would hide in caves or under bluffs to protect themselves.

After a long and difficult fight, the Missouri troops saw a white flag of truce waving through the air when they broke for a meal. On July 3, late on a sunny afternoon, General Grant met with General Pemberton. General Pemberton wanted to know the terms of surrender, and Grant stated that surrender must be unconditional. General Pemberton had a difficult decision to make that night.

In the first morning light of July 4, the Confederate troops at Vicksburg abandoned their weapons and surrendered the town to the Union. They had successfully held the city for forty-seven days, and although they had not lost a single battle, they were no longer able to keep the Union from taking the city.

In the days following the surrender, the Confederate

troops were held by the Union army, and Bounds found himself once again a prisoner. It would not be a long-term imprisonment: The men would be paroled in exchange for captured Union soldiers. While they awaited parole, the duties of the chaplains were considerably lighter. Several of the chaplains had the opportunity to return to Missouri. Sadly, that was not an option for Bounds, who was still restricted by the banishment order that had sent him to the South in the first place. He was pleased that he would be able to send letters to his family through the men traveling to their area.

Prisoners were officially paroled just a few short days later, and Bounds once again found himself following the call of the Lord. Prayer had begun to fully infiltrate Bounds's lifestyle, and at every turn he sought the Lord's will. Though saddened by the events of the war and disturbed by the constant state of fighting, Bounds pressed forward in an effort to be a light to those around him.

Even as the tides of war began to turn and it grew increasingly apparent that the Union would gain victory, Bounds remained a support system for the men he served.

Toward the end of the war, Bounds was stationed in the city of Franklin, Tennessee. This city had endured a long, painful battle that resulted in a devastating Confederate loss. Bounds remained on the front lines through the battle and was deeply grieved at the losses that were suffered. Word came that Nashville had fallen to the Union and that men still physically able would need to reinforce the retreating Confederacy troops.

There were a great many soldiers wounded and suffering in Franklin. Bounds made the difficult decision to stay behind and minister to those in the gravest of pain, rather than travel on ahead with the reinforcements. A little later the Union troops officially took over the city of Franklin, classifying Bounds and the wounded men as captured.

Allowed to remain on and minister in Franklin, Bounds found a civilian population in need of his help. During the war they had not been able to maintain regular church services, and the people were in need of fellowship and preaching. Bounds began holding prayer meetings with a few of the men, which spread into hosting Bible studies in different homes as an outreach for those in need.

When all the wounded soldiers were well enough to be shipped, they were transferred to Nashville along with Bounds. Held in the stockade on the public square, Bounds was ever faithful in his prayers for the soldiers and the country. The last remaining hope for a Southern victory flickered out when General Grant's plan to cut off all supply lines to the South began to take effect. On March 17, Bounds was again offered the opportunity to pledge his allegiance to the United States of America. This time, he gave his oath. On April 9, 1865, Robert E. Lee officially surrendered to Ulysses S. Grant at Appomattox Court House, Virginia.

The surrender did not immediately secure Bounds his release. Word spread slowly through the cities and even slower to the men on the battlefield. Finally, on June 28, 1865, Bounds was able to pledge his allegiance to the country and was released from custody. His banishment order, however, was still in effect until all skirmishes died down. Bounds had to agree to not return to Missouri until word had sufficiently spread that the war was over.

Years of witnessing such tragic events and terrible warfare had taken its toll on Bounds. He had learned the value of human life and the necessity of prayer. On the battlefield and in his travels, Bounds had learned the art of constant submission to the Lord and faith that his prayers would be heard. Many left the war disillusioned by what they had seen and angry at the Lord. Bounds left with a peace that God had carried him through the most troubling time in his life and sustained him with the fellowship of the Spirit.

seven

Bounds had spent four long years serving faithfully in the position of chaplain, but those years wore him out, and he was in much need of rest and rejuvenation. Almost thirty years old, he hoped to begin settling into a town once again and picking up his ministry without the trauma of the battlefield. It was a joyful day when the people of Franklin, much beloved by Bounds, invited him back to the small Methodist church as their pastor.

The return to Franklin was a delight for Bounds, yet it was not without its difficulties. The task of reconstruction was creating many problems. Flare-ups between former Confederate supporters and Union soldiers abounded. In his quiet yet firm manner, Bounds did his best to ease the problems, preaching the importance of reconciliation and love for one's neighbors.

Colonel Opedyke of the 125th Ohio Volunteer Infantry was amazed by the life Bounds led. He saw Bounds show compassion to Union soldiers, even though he still dressed in Confederate gray. Opedyke could see the true depth of concern that Bounds had for all people and realized that Bounds was far more effective than his own chaplains. Opedyke scheduled a meeting with Bounds.

"We have occupied the church house and land since March 1862, but now I will be moving my troops to a new area so that your ministry will again have a meeting place," Opedyke explained to Bounds.

Bounds was deeply moved by the impact he had on the colonel. The Union troops were moved out the very next day, and the town of Franklin reclaimed its church.

As the months passed and the Union continued to occupy their city, the citizens of Franklin grew resentful and restless. Bounds preached often on the importance of a pure and loving heart and on the godly principle of loving others above ourselves. During that time he was named to the office of elder within the Tennessee Methodist Conference. The people of Franklin were joyful at the announcement and planned to host a community wide dinner in Bounds's honor. The dinner plans were reminiscent of the old camp meetings that had spread revival through the country. In an effort to mimic the camp meetings, they put the event off to gain sufficient time to plan.

The people began to gather in prayer groups, their hearts burdened for others in their community. After fifteen long months of deep prayer and petitioning, revival swept the church. Within weeks, 150 people had committed themselves to Christ and were seeking to walk with the Lord. Amazed at the work God was doing within the community, Bounds and his flock rejoiced with the new believers as they all worshiped together.

The church continued to grow, and it became increasingly necessary to have a larger meeting place. Plans were drawn up and land was purchased. Much to everyone's delight, in April 1868, ground was broken on their new building site.

Although Bounds was pivotal in the planning of the building, he was not able to remain for the completion of the project. He had been called by his conference to pastor in Selma, Alabama. The people of Franklin, who held Bounds in the highest esteem, were saddened to have him leave, even as their new pastor arrived. Bounds encouraged them on the Lord's perfect timing and exhorted them to continue to follow the path God set before them. Quickly adjusting to the change, Bounds left Franklin for Selma with great expectancy for what the Lord would call him to next.

The people of Selma remembered Bounds from the revival that had broken out about six years earlier in their area, during the spring of 1863. They were delighted to have him back and greeted him with kindness and respect. The town was not as Bounds remembered it. He was moved to the point of tears as he walked through the city and surrounding areas, both of which had been devastated in the war.

There was one area in particular that Bounds felt a heavy burden toward. Living among the rubble of the old Confederate naval foundry were families with nowhere else to go, many of them freed slaves who had no way to gain employment. Bounds brought these families' needs before the congregation, which set out to do whatever they could to help.

Bounds remained in Selma for three years, preaching and ministering to the needs of the community. Although he loved the people of Selma and the ministry opportunities he had there, his new assignment came through, and Bounds was again excited to see where God would use him next.

Now thirty-six, Bounds was assigned to the First Methodist Episcopal Church South in Eufaula, Alabama. Although Selma had many lasting after-effects of war, Eufaula was ripped apart and had yet to find a way of reconciliation. Arriving at his new church, Bounds, full of compassion for the city and its people, began praying for the Spirit of God to claim the hearts of the citizens.

Eufaula was plagued by crime on a daily basis. Robberies, assaults, and even murders had become commonplace. The police could not keep a steady peace, and the turmoil had destroyed much of the

Christian base the city once had. Knowing that the city's problems would not be fixed overnight, Bounds set out to make his life a living witness to those around him. His righteous lifestyle raised the standards of the church community and began to have an effect on the lives of his flock.

Bounds found that one particular problem was the newspaper, which created more conflict than news. Bounds challenged the paper to allow him to place a weekly editorial column in the paper. By God's grace, the newspaper agreed, and Bounds's ministry through the written word officially began. His column addressed issues with integrity and intelligence. He avoided pointing fingers and instead looked for realistic solutions to the city's problems. By the end of the year, Bounds's column was printed not only in Eufaula but was featured in newspapers across Alabama and Georgia.

Though the city of Eufaula continued to be plagued with racial issues and angry hearts, Bounds continued to pray and encourage, knowing that God was at work even when it wasn't easily apparent.

In the early months of summer, Bounds was preaching at a funeral service for a local family. Seeing a woman he termed "the most beautiful woman in the world," he discreetly inquired about her. He was told her name was Emma Elizabeth Barnett and she had recently returned to the area after an extended stay with her cousins in Georgia. Though Bounds did not directly pursue her at that time, she remained in the forefront of his thoughts as he went about his ministry.

Shortly thereafter, Bounds received the sad news of his sister's death. His mother asked him to come back home to Missouri. The skirmishes that had kept his banishment order in place had since died out, and he was free to travel home for the first time in many years. It was, of course, a bittersweet reunion as he bid farewell to his sister while greeting the remaining members of his family. Encouraged by his family's support and the fellowship of his hometown, Bounds returned to Eufaula with a fresh vision and a renewed sense of purpose in his ministry.

The membership numbers of Bounds's church in Eufaula had been steadily increasing during his ministry, and it became necessary to build a larger meeting place. After weighing the options, the church community decided that a full relocation was best. In the meantime they would meet for services in Hart Hall. Not wanting to build a new church building that would leave the congregation struggling to get out of debt, Bounds set up programs for donations and drives that would allow them to pay for the building as it was built.

That was a unique idea at the time, and there were many newspaper articles referring to the integrity and honor that Bounds infused into the church. During the building, Bounds continued his newspaper writing, and his impact continued to expand as more newspapers began printing his articles.

On April 4, 1875, the new church building was officially dedicated, much to the delight of all who had participated in its construction. Bounds himself was overjoyed not only with the building, but with the growth it represented. In the four years between his arrival and the completion of the building, the church went from 180 adults and children involved in Bible studies to 280 adults and children involved in Bible studies. That growth was a great joy for Bounds.

The fall of 1875 arrived, and Bounds was once again called in a new direction. This time he was presented with an opportunity to return to Missouri, specifically the city of St. Louis. Bounds grew quickly attached to his new congregation and felt incredibly blessed by the opportunities God had set out for him.

There was but one thing missing from life in St. Louis—the beautiful Emma Barnett. Letters passed swiftly back and forth between the two, and soon Bounds was once again on the train to Eufaula.

"I love you and I want you with me forever," Bounds professed upon his return to Eufaula. After visiting with Emma and finding she felt the same way, he sought the approval of her father, which he received. While plans for the wedding were being made, Bounds returned to St. Louis and his work. On September 19, 1876, Edward McKendree Bounds married Emma Elizabeth Barnett at the First Methodist Church of Eufaula, the church Bounds had been so influential in building.

Returning to St. Louis together, Bounds presented his new wife to the congregation amid much joy and celebration. Although she was only twenty-one to his forty-one years, she was welcomed warmly, and the new Bounds family settled into a life of ministry and marriage.

The life and ministry of E. M. Bounds continued to flourish. He was blessed with sons and daughters whom he loved wholeheartedly and sought to raise in the understanding of the Lord. He suffered the tragic loss of his wife and spent many years grieving her absence. Later he was blessed with a second happy marriage that carried him through the end of his life.

As time went on, God began to call Bounds in a different direction. Although he had a heart for the people in his congregation, he also developed a passion for sharing the truths he had learned through writing. Moving from newspaper articles to books, Bounds was able to greatly expand his ministry through his powerful works on the subject of prayer. Prayer had changed his own life and ministry. Bounds desired others to have that understanding as well. His books live on today as a testimony to all he learned through the trying and joyful times of his life and leave a legacy of devotion and love for the Lord.

GEORGE
FOX

one

George Fox felt, from the time he was a young boy, that he needed to escape the often oppressive nature of his home life. His father, suffering the pain of an amputated leg, was almost always on the dangerous edge of anger. With his quick temper and sharp tongue, he was not the kindest of parents. "Boys, quiet down and behave," he would often order. "Get that work done. There's too much work to spend the day playing around."

There was little time for fun in the Fox household. George did not enjoy the strict standards his father demanded of him and his siblings, but he sought to adhere to them the best he could.

Fox's mother, a strong woman of German descent, became apt at keeping the children out of their father's hair. She had four sons and one daughter, all of whom kept her on her toes and busy organizing the household and their individual needs. She was a woman of deep faith and regular church worship. Her life, including the reading and application of God's Word, stood as an example to Fox as he matured into his teen years.

"George, come and hear this verse. Listen to what God is saying to us today." She would beckon him over to learn from the Bible whenever there was time.

"Never stray from what the Lord has taught us," she would instruct, teaching her children to walk in a path pleasing to the Lord. His mother was a light to the family, and her faith in God was an encouragement to them all.

As Fox grew older, he found that it became more and more difficult to live under the strict, demanding rules his father put forth. He found escape in the form of a makeshift library. A childless neighborhood couple, the Kruezpointers, turned part of their home into a library for the neighborhood children. Fox found the stories he read and the freedom he had there an overwhelming relief from the routine at home. Late at night in the small attic room he shared with his three brothers, he thought of the stories he read and knew that someday soon he would have to get out and see the world for himself.

In 1917 America declared war on Germany. Newspapers highlighted the action of battle and the movement of troops; men hurried to enlist; and the buzz of the nation was on what would happen next. Fox grew increasingly restless in his desire to join the war effort. He was, however, only seventeen and would not be able to enlist without his parents' consent. Fearing they would never allow him to go, Fox wondered what he should do.

After a few days of thought, Fox found himself standing on the sidewalk outside the recruitment center. It took a few moments and a lot of nerve, but he finally walked inside. Knowing that he would need to appear every bit his age if he were to pull this off, he held his head high and met the stare of the men inside with easy confidence.

"Name and birth date," the officer in charge required of him as paperwork was filled out all around him.

"George Lansing Fox," he answered. After a brief pause, he continued, "and I was born in 1898."

Fox had pushed his birth date back a year so it would seem he was eighteen. The lie made him uncomfortable, but he pressed on in his determination to be out of his house and into the war. The officer in charge wanted to see a birth certificate, but Fox talked his way around that request, and within the hour he was officially enrolled as a soldier.

Fox was informed that he would be leaving the following morning, giving him one last night at home. Deciding not to inform his family of what he had done, he returned home for dinner as if it were just another day. He spent the evening with new awareness, taking in everything around him. He knew that he would likely never come back to that house—at least not in the near future. He appreciated having one more evening with his mother, and although he was not close to his siblings, he also tried to enjoy one last evening with them.

The next morning Fox prepared for the day as if he were leaving for work, with the clothes on his back and a toothbrush in his pocket. He had very little money, but he took what he had in hopes of rationing it out over time. Saying a quick good-bye to his mother as he walked out the door, Fox headed to his new destination without even looking back.

George had a small nagging feeling that his mother deserved an explanation, but he also knew the kind of trouble such an explanation would create within the careful balance of the household. He planned to write her a letter as soon as possible so she would not worry unnecessarily. It was not the best solution, but as he walked down the street and away from his childhood home he trusted that his mother's faith would carry her through. He personally was not even tempted to look back. Every step away from home brought freedom, and that freedom called to him with a cry too loud to ignore and too strong to turn away.

two

As he grew up, George Fox had watched his mother endure a difficult lifestyle and turbulent financial situation by turning to God. In his early days of army training, Fox learned for himself the personal value of turning to God. He carried with him the memories of his mother, her head bent in prayer, seeking to love the Lord in all her life.

That image sustained him in a way he could not express, and as the days turned to nights and the nights turned back to days, Fox began to bow his head in prayer. He sought God in his day-to-day life and began reading from a small pocket New Testament he acquired somewhere along the way. The early seeds of faith planted by his mother and harvested through the situations of his life took root in those early army days. At the time, he had no idea just how significant a change he was making in that act of prayer and discovery of God's Word.

While the training was difficult, Fox found that he enjoyed the discipline and drive that pushed the troops forward. He had entered the army in good physical condition, and although it was not always easy, he found that the drills and marches were not as difficult for him as they were for many other new recruits. He began to build friendships, strengthened by the intensity of what the men were sharing. His growth in the Lord, physical training, and new relationships came together and allowed Fox to find enjoyment and peace amid the strenuous activities of training.

An answer to prayer came in the form of his post-training assignment. Fox was capable of filling many positions, but he felt a heavy burden at the thought of taking the lives of others, even in battle. He would do his duty if called to do so, but there was no excitement at such an idea.

He felt blessed to be assigned to the ambulance corps, an assignment that would allow him to be of service to his fellow soldiers, rather than an enemy against an opposing army. He knew there were many dangers to the assignment which required him to remain on the front line, but he was at peace about that.

George spoke to the men around him, telling them of the verse in Joshua 1:5 that proclaims, "There shall not any man be able to stand before thee all the days of thy life: as I was with Moses, so I will be with thee:

I will not fail thee, nor forsake thee." Fox took great comfort in the knowledge of God's presence and provision and sought to share that comfort with those around him.

Not many days later, Fox was shipped to Camp Baker, Texas. There he was trained in the specialized skills of the ambulance corps, not the least of which was the ability to drive an ambulance. Not many from his hometown had known how to drive, but like any young man, Fox was thrilled at the opportunity to learn.

Fox was also trained in the basics of first aid on the battlefield and how to set up treatment centers. It was important that Fox's group trained together because they would be working together in the field, and good teamwork could be the difference between life and death. The ambulances were supposed to be safe from enemy fire, but when working around enemy fire, no one was truly safe.

"What do you think New York City will be like?" Fox wondered the evening before they were to be transferred to New York. The soldiers would be held over there for a few days before shipping out to their destination in France.

"Busy. Full of glamor and important people," another soldier chimed in, also considering what their time in the city would bring.

As it turned out, the young men had nearly three full days in the city to explore, and they found it was indeed a busy place full of excitement and adventure.

Fox loved the city and hoped that he would be able to return someday and enjoy the sights again. Many of the other soldiers agreed, and en route to France they dreamed of the day when the war would be over and they would return. Heavy on their hearts was the realization that they would not all be returning—that the battlefield would likely claim at least some of their lives. They did not dwell on it, though. Instead they focused on the enjoyable time they had and their hopes for a bright future.

Soon the reality of life and death overtook the soldiers aboard the ship. Traveling on the *Huron*, Fox soon found that sickness spread quickly in a crowded area. A flu epidemic spread through the soldiers, claiming the lives of two men. It was a troubling time, and the loss laid heavily on the hearts of the men who survived the illness. The sickness was like a stench that just would not go away. It haunted the men throughout the entire trip, striking some and then disappearing, only to flare up again later. The soldiers arrived in France with tired bodies and saddened spirits.

Fox spent his first assignment in field hospitals well behind the front lines. The soldiers they treated and transferred were in grave pain but not straight from the battlefield. They were often given treatment somewhere else before being moved back to the hospital where Fox was stationed. The pain and severity of their injuries were staggering, and Fox felt a constant need to turn to the Lord amid such disturbing sights and sounds.

Word arrived that Fox would be moved immediately to the front lines, to the field hospital in Ventri, which was near Chaumont and the American headquarters. This new assignment taught Fox the true depth of pain and suffering that comes in the midst of war. He worked day and night tending the wounded and bringing new patients back from the front lines. The men were in horrible shape. Many had lost limbs; others had been caught in explosions and suffered from severe burns; and still others were nearly unidentifiable. Fox worked diligently, doing his best for the men and trying to find a sense of peace for himself amid the tragedies that surrounded him.

When his spiritual pain was excruciating and he hadn't slept in days, Fox depended on the Lord. He kept his pocket New Testament with him, wearing it out as he leaned on the Lord. The strength he found in his relationship with God sustained him through the terrible experiences of war, and he was known for sharing that strength whenever an opportunity arose.

One fateful day in November would forever change the course of Fox's life. He had been sent to set up a new field hospital in Giraucourt on November 10, 1918. In the middle of the setup, loud explosions were followed by tremendous crashing sounds. Artillery shells were hitting the building that Fox had been working on. The roof split, and the walls came crashing down. An array of bricks and other debris toppled over Fox as he attempted to duck for cover.

The world slowly faded to black, and the weight of the bricks fell upon him.

He awoke days later, unsure of his surroundings. "Help!" he cried in confusion, feeling the pain and realizing that he was in a hospital.

"Sir, you must lay still," a nurse quickly said as Fox attempted to sit up. The pain shooting through his body was like nothing he had ever felt before, and he wondered how he was alive.

"What happened?" he begged in desperation, needing to know what had done this to him.

"Your back was broken in the collapse of the building," the nurse explained.

Through many months of frustration and pain, Fox had to relearn how to walk. It was a difficult time in his life. He questioned what the events meant to him and why it had happened. During that time, his heart was once again opened to his family and what they meant to him. Through the mail he was able to get in touch with them again, and they began to form a closer connection. The family had moved to a farm since George left, which was not anything he was interested in doing, but while he didn't intend to join them, he greatly appreciated his renewed relationships with them.

Fox knew he did not intend to go home, but he had no idea of what he did intend to do. He was in a difficult position when it came to the future. He had never finished high school and had very limited skills outside of his army training. Added to that was his injury, which left him with a 29 percent partial disability. He was once again able to walk on his own, but where could he go?

three

Fox returned to America in 1919, still confused as to what he should do next. He knew that no matter what, he needed to complete his education and find a job that allowed him to support himself. He did just that, working days at Guarantee Title and Trust Company and spending his nights completing the classes he needed to finish high school. During this time of transition he began to feel a call to full-time ministry.

Years of war had taught Fox many things about trusting in the Lord and what is truly important in life. As the call became stronger, he began to see that he could have a real impact on those God placed in his life. He had tried his best throughout the war to witness to the soldiers working with him, but there was little time for talk amid the fighting and the plight of the injured. The desire to live out that ministry and share the love of the Lord with others on a daily basis laid heavily on Fox's heart.

In 1923 Fox got together enough money and the needed education to enroll in Moody Bible Institute, located in Chicago. This would involve a move from New York to Chicago, but he considered it well worth the effort for the education he would obtain at a school with a stellar reputation. As it turned out, the move was a great opportunity in more ways than one.

When Fox met Isadora Hurlbut he knew in an instant that she was the woman he wanted to marry. She was charming and kind, funny and compassionate, and her love for the Lord flowed out of her actions with ease. Isadora, on the other hand, was not so instantly enamored. This led to many months of romantic pursuit. As time passed, they discovered that they truly did have much in common and began to spend some time together. Before they knew it, they were discussing engagement rings.

The engagement period was not to be an easy time for either of the two young people. Isadora came from a well-to-do family in Vermont, and they were not too sure about her plans to marry. Her sister especially was concerned with Fox's status as a disabled veteran, because it could make for difficult times if he needed further care. When they visited her family, Fox became increasingly aware of the scrutiny, and his nervousness soared. This made matters worse, and by the end of the visit Isadora was questioning her decision to marry him.

In a hasty, emotional decision, Isadora broke off the engagement. For the first time in a long time, Fox felt completely unsure of the direction of his life. He was nearly finished with his education and thought the marriage plans were going on without a problem. Isadora also struggled with the decision she made. Less than a full day later, she was in near hysterics, regretting the decision. She took to her knees in prayer, asking God for another chance and knowing that if she could, she would spend the rest of her life married to George Fox. Fox had spent much time in prayer as well. Fortunately he was unwilling to walk away from the relationship without a struggle. He went to see her that very night, and after much discussion they not only decided to marry, but they moved the wedding date up by six full months! Now they were both sure of what they wanted.

The early years of marriage were not always easy, often filled with money problems and family issues. Yet, through everything, the two remained strong together; they trusted in God and sought to live their lives in a way that pleased the Lord. Fox graduated from the Bible Institute but was not immediately able to go into full-time ministry. Jobs were scarce at the time, and the vocation of a pastor was not easily obtained. He took up several part-time accounting jobs to pay the rent and take care of his new bride.

Those years taught the young couple many things, including how to trust one another and lean on the Lord for all things.

On November 11, 1924, Fox was overjoyed by the birth of his first child, a son they named Wyatt. The year before, Isadora had miscarried in the first few months of her pregnancy. Although Wyatt would never be a replacement for the lost child, they knew a deep sense of relief when she delivered a healthy baby boy.

Two years after the birth of his son, Fox was blessed with the opportunity to go into full-time ministry. He was accepted into the Vermont Conference of the Methodist Church and assigned to pastor the West Berkshire circuit. This was an exciting time for Fox, who now headed up two churches, the East Franklin and West Franklin of West Berkshire, Vermont. He found himself enthralled with the work of the Lord and knew a true sense of peace in putting his accounting jobs aside to focus on the people of his churches.

Fox greatly enjoyed the small churches he was ministering to. They were small farming communities near slightly busier cities. The land was quite beautiful, and the churches were lovely; however, on many occasions his small salary could not cover the monthly needs of a family. He found his congregations most helpful and eager to assist their diligent pastor in any way they were able.

Fox's family continued to expand. On January 29,

1928, his second child was born. Mary Elizabeth was born to them after a long and trying labor. The joy of a second child soon overshadowed the troublesome labor as the family adjusted to a second child in the household.

The following years were full of many adjustments and changes. Fox transitioned back into school, furthering his education and allowing for greater opportunities. They lived in a number of different places while he went to school in Boston and worked to support his family. Those years were a wonderful time of spiritual growth. They were also a delightful time for the young couple, who loved watching Wyatt and Mary begin to grow up. Times were not always easy in the Fox household, but God is good, and they were always provided with the necessities they needed, even if all of their wants could not be filled. It mattered not in the big scheme of things. The most important parts of life to Fox and his wife were serving the Lord and raising their family, both of which they did with great enthusiasm and commitment.

four

Time passed swiftly and, in what seemed like months instead of years, the Fox children reached high school. The family had a special bond and unity that delighted George, who had come from such a disjointed family. The only major issue that arose centered around their financial situation.

As a minister, Fox's highest salary was $1,425 plus the parsonage. This was in the 1930s. It was painfully low pay, and during the depression years it dipped even lower. Fox felt that necessities were justified but extras should be done without. One day his son declared in frustration, "I will never become a minister. I would never put my family through this!" Fox understood his son's opinion of their lifestyle and attempted to loosen the purse-strings whenever possible. He felt, however, that there was no greater reward than to serve the Lord in a full-time capacity, and he had no intention of leaving the ministry.

When money was not being discussed, the family enjoyed good relationships. Wyatt and Mary, though certainly not perfect, got along well and were respectful of their parents. In turn, their parents allowed them responsibilities and trusted them to make wise decisions. Family vacations were an exciting time. They would venture out to see family in Vermont and stay with Isadora's sister and her family. The children loved the change, and Fox was always glad to return to Vermont, which was one of his favorite places.

Just shortly before such a trip to Lyndonville, the news reported the bombing of Pearl Harbor. The event shocked the nation. Many young men were inspired to join the armed forces and defend their country. Wyatt, who was completing his senior year of high school, began thinking and planning when he would graduate and when he should enlist.

Wyatt was not the only member of the Fox family stirred by the chilling reports of Pearl Harbor. The news struck deeply within Fox, who had experienced the first of the world wars just decades before.

The night they heard the news, he paced the floor and contemplated what his role in the coming war should be. His heart was burdened for the young men who had no idea what they were about to experience, and he knew they would be gravely in need of spiritual guidance as they experienced the horrors of war.

Fox decided to join the Chaplain Corps of the United States Army. This time, though, instead of trying to offer spiritual guidance between the many jobs he was doing, his only responsibility would be to mentor the young soldiers and lead them in their spiritual journey. The prospects delighted Fox, although the idea of leaving his family behind was a difficult one to handle. He trusted that no matter what, the Lord would be with them all.

While away at the Middlebury Midwinter Conference for the American Legion Department of Vermont (of which Fox was the chaplain), Fox slipped away for an afternoon to Albany, New York. Wyatt had joined him for the conference and traveled to Albany with his father. Both men enlisted in the armed forces that afternoon. Wyatt enlisted in the Marine Corps for a four-year term that would start upon graduation from high school. He passed all the examinations and was admitted to the program. Fox also signed papers that day, quietly working to receive a position as an army chaplain.

Fox went to Washington, D.C., to go before the Methodist Commission on Chaplains and obtain permission to apply for a commission in the United States Army Chaplains. The time in Washington went quite well. Now Fox needed to pass his physical exam. There were some lingering doubts in his mind as to whether he would be able to pass after the injuries he had sustained in the first war, yet he pressed on.

That Easter, Fox preached what was considered one of the most inspiring and moving sermons the parish had ever heard. His wife was greeted fondly as people spoke of how touching his words were to their hearts and minds.

It was a sad day for Wyatt. He spent a portion of the afternoon in tears in his room, knowing his father's sermon could very well be the last Easter sermon he would hear his father preach. He expressed that thought to his mother, who had experienced a similar thought that morning.

On June 12, 1942, Wyatt Fox graduated from high school. His proud parents and younger sister looked on from their seats in the audience, applauding his work and encouraging him in his drive to pursue his goals in the Marines.

A week later, Wyatt left for boot camp. It was a difficult day for the close family, which did not know when or if they would ever be together again. At the train station, Wyatt leaped into his father's arms. "I love you!" he said with great emotion.

"I love you, too, and my prayers will go with you," Fox assured his son. It was an emotional, tear-filled good-bye as the men parted company, each to serve the country in his own way.

Not very long after that, Fox received word that he had been accepted as a chaplain and needed to report to a one-month training conference at Harvard College. Fox, his wife, and their daughter arrived at

Harvard on August 4, 1942, and by September 5 he had completed his training. They were sent to Camp Davis, North Carolina. Fox worked diligently there, although part of him hoped he would receive an opportunity to minister closer to the front lines.

Nine weeks after arriving in North Carolina, Fox was informed that he would be shipping up to Camp Miles Standish in Massachusetts. It was a difficult time for his wife, who could only stay with him on the weekends, and for his daughter, who was in her senior year of high school and adjusting to the third move in a matter of months. They did the best they could under the circumstances.

Isadora and Mary were able to see Fox on the weekends, and he came to visit them as often as possible. It was not the ideal situation, but Fox felt strongly that God was using him for the good of the soldiers and knew that he was where he belonged. Isadora struggled when she learned that his name appeared high on the list of those slated to be shipped overseas, but she looked to God and held firmly in her faith, even when the situation was distressing.

The Fox's nineteenth wedding anniversary arrived during this time, and he surprised Isadora with nineteen red roses and a special visit. They spent the weekend together celebrating their marriage and trying to keep thoughts of war from their minds.

Fox was scheduled to leave for the base early Monday morning. Both knew there was a good chance he would not be back before shipping out overseas. Isadora wanted to walk him to the bus station, but he insisted she remain in the house.

"I would rather leave you here in the home that I am coming back to," he informed her gently as they stood at the door. After kissing him good-bye, Isadora watched him slowly walk away until he disappeared into the early morning fog.

five

Shortly after arriving in Massachusetts, Fox met three other chaplains who would become his companions and confidants through all that was to come. The men were Clark Poling, Father John Washington, and Rabbi Alex Goode. Their faiths did not always meet on common ground, but the men worked together as a team to help the soldiers they served.

The four chaplains were assigned to ship out aboard the *Dorchester*, although their orders were sealed, and they did not know where they were going until they arrived in New York Harbor to board the ship. The *Dorchester* was not what they expected. It was clearly smaller than most of the other ships in the harbor, but it had survived five trips across the Atlantic so far that year and proven its worth on the open sea.

The *Dorchester* possessed an interesting history. It was not originally intended as a warship but had been used in transporting goods and passengers up and down the East Coast. The outbreak of war created a great need for available ships, and the *Dorchester* was commissioned by the navy to help in the war effort.

The men boarded the ship together, exploring their living quarters and realizing that it would be a very crowded voyage. The ship had seen better days. It was in perfect working condition, but there were much-needed maintenance jobs waiting throughout the living quarters. It was also quickly apparent that there were a large number of men shipping out—over double the typical maximum capacity—which would create even tighter quarters.

"Well, the men won't be able to avoid us!" Fox joked as they settled in.

The following morning the four chaplains, who held the rank of lieutenants, were summoned, along with the other officers, to meet Captain Danielsen. The meeting overflowed the captain's quarters. Between twenty and thirty men were in attendance, all waiting eagerly to find out where they were going and what was to happen next. As the meeting began, the ship made its way slowly out of the harbor toward the open sea.

"This will not be a typical voyage," the captain began. "This has been apparent already in the mysterious way in which you arrived and the lack of details you have all received. You are not the only ones, though, lacking in detail. I have not yet been informed of our mission or destination."

The seriousness of the mission began to sink in. Fox knew that the coming time would be a time of trial but also a great opportunity. His heart was already in prayer for the men aboard the ship and how he would best be able to minister to their needs.

Sealed orders were opened once the ship was officially out at sea. They instructed the *Dorchester* to proceed to St. John's, Newfoundland, where further instructions would be given. The mission was still a mystery, and real-life mysteries lead to nervousness, often danger. The very real threat of German U-boats seeking them out already hung heavily over the ship. The awareness of such possibilities was high, even though everyone tried not to think about it.

"The men are young, unseasoned, and scared. Your guidance is very necessary to their lives, even if they don't yet realize it," the captain explained to the chaplains over lunch in his quarters.

"We certainly plan on helping them any way we can," Fox responded, glad that the captain was open to their work aboard his ship.

"I'm glad to hear it. This is the first time we've taken chaplains aboard such a trip, and now we've got four. I'd say there's a divine reason for such a switch, and I'll look forward to seeing how things work out," the captain told the men, not really sure why so many chaplains had been assigned to this voyage.

The men finished their lunch together, speaking of home and their lives before the war. The four chaplains were getting along well, even in their tight quarters, and the captain enjoyed the easy conversation among them. The meal ended with a brief time of prayer for the voyage ahead and the hearts of the men aboard the ship.

Fox began to join the men at meals and any other time they had a few moments to relax. Although icy weather kept many from going out on the deck, there were staterooms where the men could gather when they needed to get out of their tight cabins. The chaplains had discussed it, and they wanted to be around for the men as much as possible. They felt that the more visible they were around the ship, the more comfortable the men would feel coming to them with spiritual issues. The intensity of their mission formed a swift bond between the men, and it did indeed prove to be a springboard to spiritual discussions. It also allowed men to come to them when they just needed someone to talk to about the fears they were facing or the homesickness they were feeling.

The first two days at sea required some adjusting. Fox struggled to sleep, trying to ignore the constant hum of the engines and the motion of the ship, but the mood aboard the ship the first two days was generally lively. The men were anticipating what was to come and feeling fairly secure. But the closer the ship came to Newfoundland, the closer they were to the U-boats, and the mood aboard ship became sober. The third day dawned cold and dreary, full of rain and clouds. The mood of the soldiers was not much better, and Fox sensed that they were struggling to keep their faith and hopes alive.

"Son, how's it going today?" Fox inquired of a young soldier at breakfast.

"Everything's great," the soldier quickly responded. After the brief response, the young man ducked his head and focused steadily on his plate of food.

Fox sat watching the young soldier and felt a deep yearning for his own son. Wyatt had not been able to get in touch with him before they shipped out, so Fox was no longer sure where his son was stationed or what he was doing. What Fox did know was that he would want someone to be there for Wyatt as he was there for the young man before him. Fox sat silently praying for a few moments, both for Wyatt and for the young man before him.

"Do you think we'll make it?" The young man's question broke through Fox's silent prayers.

"What do you think?" Fox asked in return.

"I think those U-boats know what they're doing, and if they get their sights set on us there's nothing we can do about it."

Fox nodded slightly, knowing there was truth to the soldier's statement. "I suppose that's right. But I'd like to think that it's not those U-boats with the power, but

God Almighty, who knows what's going to happen and will see us through anything."

"You think God's watching out for us?" the soldier asked, staring intently at the chaplain. The soldier wanted very much to believe that he would be taken care of, but the tight quarters of the ship and the fear that seemed to hang in the air were suffocating the hope right out of him.

"Always. Maybe not always the way we want, but God is always here," Fox explained.

"Chaplain, you think you could pray for me?" the soldier asked, and then tentatively ducked his head again.

"Son, I'd be honored," Fox answered before bowing his head and lifting his heart to the Lord in prayer.

Later that day, the four chaplains were talking about the emotional state of the men. The mood throughout the ship was similar to that of the young man Fox had prayed for. Men who had boarded the ship with faith were struggling to maintain it. Men who were still seeking what they believed were struggling even more. The chaplains came together in prayer, knowing that they needed to do something to lift the mood of the soldiers and help them prepare for whatever was ahead.

"A party, something that will lift the men's spirits and help them come together," one of the chaplains suggested. The others swiftly agreed that a party would be the perfect solution. It could be a time to gather and relax without the pressure of an official religious service.

"We can check with the captain and get started," the chaplains decided, hurrying off to get permission.

The captain agreed that the party was a wonderful idea. He had seen the sagging spirits of the soldiers. They would be arriving in Newfoundland the following morning, and he needed them to be ready for whatever the next leg of their mission was. With the captain's permission, the chaplains set out to prepare the stateroom with makeshift decorations and prepare some forms of entertainment.

"I heard there's some party going on tonight," a soldier mentioned to the others surrounding him in his tight quarters below deck.

"Yeah, I heard that, too," another one chimed in. "You going?" he asked.

"I don't know. It's those chaplains' idea."

Another soldier chimed in. "So what, man? A party's a party, and I'm all for getting out of here and kicking back for a few hours."

The first soldier stated, "Me, too." Others quickly chimed in, and soon word had spread throughout the ship.

The stateroom was soon teeming with soldiers, and the men were once again relaxed and hopeful. The three days aboard ship had been stressful, and everyone agreed it was nice to relax and unwind.

Fox walked through the room, greeting those he

knew and attempting to make the acquaintance of others.

"Hey, Chaplain Fox," a voice called out from behind him. Turning, Fox saw the young soldier whom he had breakfast with that morning.

"How's it going, son?" Fox asked as he shook the man's hand.

"Good. And you know what? This time I mean it," he responded with a grin.

"Well now, that's good to hear." Fox broke into a smile.

"Yeah. When I got back to my room I thought about what you said about God. I pulled out this little New Testament I have, and there's actually some great stuff in there!" Fox felt a deep sense of joy over this young man and the impact he had been able to have on his life. They talked for a while before Chaplain Washington began to speak.

Fox took the opportunity to stand back slightly from the crowd and pray for the men, that they would have open hearts and ears. He prayed for Washington, praising God for the opportunity to share his faith and asking that he find the right words for the men before him. The chaplains were overjoyed to have the opportunity to not only lift the men's spirits with a party, but to use the opportunity to speak directly about the Lord.

The night was long with singing, and eventually the men had to be ordered back to their bunks for some sleep. Fox, his back aching from the motion of the ship and the activity of the past few days, crawled into bed desperate for sleep. His dreams came in flashes of memories of his wife and his children. They were always heavy in his heart and mind, and he prayed constantly for God's hand upon their lives. That night he drifted off to sleep in prayer for his family and enjoyed the pleasant dreams of memories gone by.

six

Run! Run! Go home!" The chants called out across the baseball field. The air was crisp and cold, clouds hung in the distance, but the men were finally off the ship, and nothing else mattered. They docked at a base in Newfoundland to await their next orders. Knowing they would only spend a few days there before shipping out again, the soldiers were taking every opportunity to let loose. On arrival they were restricted to certain areas of the base, and the only exercise they were getting was through their daily marches.

Fox had seen the restlessness and lingering fear of the soldiers and obtained permission to host baseball tournaments during their days onshore. Overjoyed at the activity, the men really got into the games that allowed them a chance to relax.

On the second day of the baseball tournament, all four chaplains were summoned to a special meeting aboard ship. They found a handful of officers already in the captain's area. There they received the next set of instructions for their mission.

The *Dorchester's* mission had been vague and mysterious from the moment they left shore, and finally they felt a moment of understanding was coming. Through their orders the men discovered that the *Dorchester* was carrying special technology that, when properly installed and working, would allow the Americans to locate German U-boats, saving American ships and cargo. Termed Operation Thunderbolt, the mission was vital to the war and would save thousands of lives. The ship was to continue on with the fleet to an area near Greenland. Once in Greenland, they would set up a base and establish the technology that would allow the detections to begin. This technology was top secret, and most soldiers aboard the ship would not be informed of what they were doing. It was important to keep the information from the Germans for as long as possible, and no leaks could be risked.

Fox walked slowly away from the meeting, thinking about the mission and all the lives it could save. He praised the Lord that he had the opportunity to be a part of such a glorious new wave of protection for the troops. He thought of the troublesome days still to come, because they would have to cross the main area of German U-boats in order to get to their destination. It was a risky venture, and the importance of the materials only added to the sense of seriousness in the mission. Hurrying back to the shore, Fox lifted up silent prayers that all would go safely and the technology would protect the American forces.

Soon the time on shore was completed and approximately nine hundred men were back aboard the *Dorchester*. The fleet was preparing to set sail, and the mood aboard ship was vibrant at first, but reality quickly settled around the men. They were trapped in cramped quarters and sailing through seriously dangerous waters, neither of which was easy to accept. The first day was uneventful. The men settled back into the routine of the ship. By the second day, rumors ran wild, the product of isolation and boredom. Accusations were thrown out with little thought. "I heard he's a spy." ". . .connections to Germany." "Not trustworthy. . . ." Such whisperings could be heard throughout the ship. Terms such as "spy" and "Nazi sympathizer" were being applied to men with no reason except active imaginations and uneventful days.

This was a serious morale problem, something that fell into the chaplains' area and needed to be dealt with immediately, before it became dangerous. Fox did his best to combat the gossip and slander, pointing out the loyalty the men were showing to their work and the lack of facts that all such rumors were based upon. Still the rumors persisted, and fistfights began erupting in staterooms throughout the ship.

Fox began to pray for ways to ease the tension. One of his first opportunities was a card game played by some soldiers in the stateroom.

"Room for one more?" Fox inquired lightly as he joined the men at the table.

"Of course, Chaplain," a young man responded as they made room at the table. Conversation was slow at first, but the more they played the more they began to open up. The men told Fox of their underlying fears of the "spy" aboard the ship, and how they wanted to make it back home after the war. They also expressed confusion in their faith and began to ask Fox for his opinion.

The card game was pushed aside when the conversation turned serious. The men responded well to the ideas and advice Fox shared with them. He told them of God's saving grace and a trust in the Lord that brings peace amid the worst of circumstances.

Many men aboard the ship were beginning to seek direction, so a worship service was planned for late evening on the second day back aboard the ship. It would be a wonderful opportunity for the chaplains to share the Word of the Lord and for everyone to pray for the ship and their mission.

The service, which nicely filled one of the largest rooms on board, was indeed a great time for sharing and prayer. They sang together, and a sermon was preached. Fox shared about the sacrificial love of Christ. He spoke of his family and especially his son, who was also out there somewhere serving his country. God used Fox's words to speak to the hearts of the soldiers, who left with a greater understanding of the Lord and seeking a greater purpose in their lives.

At the end of the evening they spent time in prayer for the men aboard the ship, their families back home, and all those fighting for freedom throughout the world. Fox was energized by the power of the Lord working through the hearts of the soldiers, and even as he lay in bed he could not seem to find sleep. Instead, he thought of his family and congregations back home, lifting them up to the Lord as he slowly began to drift off to sleep.

The trip from Newfoundland to Greenland was not proving to be an easy venture. Cold temperatures and rainy days combined to cover the top deck in layer after layer of ice. The deck was open to soldiers, but none really ventured out there. The ice continued to build up, and the cold air whipped across the deck, making it an increasingly unpleasant place to visit.

The conditions below deck were very much the opposite. The ship was originally designed for four hundred men but now carried just over nine hundred. It was a hot and crowded place. The men struggled in the hot, stuffy conditions, the cramped quarters, and the lack of fresh air.

Early on the second day at sea, a German U-boat was detected in range of the ship. Panic rippled through everyone's heart. Soon the U-boat turned away, and all was quiet once again. The scare led the captain to make a new order: All men were expected to wear their life jackets at all times. They were to eat, sleep, and work in the jackets, so that if the ship were hit, they would be prepared. There were enough life jackets for everyone on board, plus a few hundred extras in reserve on the deck. It was a hassle, but orders were followed and the life jackets were put on.

Fox found that his life jacket made it even more difficult to sleep. Having performed the evening service in the jacket, he longed for a few moments of relief. That was not an option. Hot and uncomfortable, he did the best he could and wore his life jacket at all times. The other chaplains were also uncomfortable but followed the orders and remained within the safety of their life jackets.

seven

There were approximately nine hours left in the journey to Greenland. Suddenly the *Dorchester* was under attack.

The men had taken to their cabins for the night, falling asleep assuming that they would be waking up to the next stage in their mission. There were 870 men in their cabins, including the captain, who had taken to his bed after a final check on the night watch. The other forty or so men were awake on night watch duty.

Those in the engine room discovered they were in the path of a U-boat, but there was nothing they could do about it. Within seconds, a torpedo had been fired at them. The men sounded the alarms, even though they knew it was too late to save themselves, and a torpedo slammed into the ship's engine room, rocking it with a heavy blast. The icy waters of the Atlantic began pouring in. The engine room lost contact with the remainder of the ship in minutes, all its crew lost in the initial blast and rush of water.

In moments, the soldiers were all scrambling from their beds and racing to the top deck while throwing on whatever clothing they could grab on their way out the door. The men gathered on the icy deck, confused and scared. Alarms continued to blare and rumors began to fly. The chaplains, as officers, went to check with the captain, to see if there was anything they could do. They soon discovered that the engine room was not responding to the captain's calls and water could be heard rushing about. The chaplains understood the seriousness of what was happening and knew there would be nothing they could do for the captain. They headed back to the top deck and their frightened soldiers.

Fox stepped onto the top deck, shocked at the sight before him. Man after man stood on the deck with no life jacket on—not just a few men, but many of the hundreds assembling on deck had no life jackets. Stopping a soldier as he rushed by in a panic, Fox asked, "Where's your safety vest, son?"

"I took it off to sleep," the young soldier cried. "I was so hot, and I just wanted to take it off, for a few minutes, but then the alarms were going off, and now it's in my cabin and I can't get back there!" The young man ran off, as if in hopes of finding a stray jacket lying on the decks somewhere. Fox realized that hundreds of the men had done exactly the same thing, and now they stood atop the deck with no life jackets.

"We've got to do something about this," Fox exclaimed to the other chaplains. "There are a few hundred extra jackets stashed throughout the ship. Many of them are in the reserves on this deck. We'll get them into some kind of order and start distributing them." Another chaplain chimed in, "Let's get started."

The air was frigid, the wind whipped wildly over the deck, and icy patches made walking a difficult task. Men without gloves quickly lost the feeling in their fingers, and the fear of hitting the icy water below sent many into a frantic state of hysteria. Quickly drafting some men to help them, the chaplains began to round up every spare life jacket they could find. Fox sent some men below deck to find as many as possible while he struggled to keep order and pass out what they did have on deck.

In addition to life jackets, the *Dorchester* was equipped with fourteen lifeboats and other emergency floats. The lifeboats and additional floatation devices were enough for more than twelve hundred passengers. The ship lurched, another explosion rocketing through the air and sending fumes over the deck. The engine room and other equipment had caught fire and would add to the speed with which the ship would sink.

Those assigned to operate and monitor the use of the lifeboats began to assemble people in the first boat. The boat was designed to hold approximately sixty passengers; it was full to the limit when the men began to lower it into the rough waters below. The ice that had formed in layers all over the deck had also frozen around the ropes holding the lifeboat. The men struggled and tried their best, but the boat lurched wildly as the ropes lowered it roughly and unevenly into the water below. The ice had done too much damage, and with no way of controlling its descent, the lifeboat capsized on entering the water. Those aboard were pulled under the rushing water. Ropes and floatation devices were thrown down. Many men were pulled back onto the ship, while others were lost too quickly as the soldiers aboard the deck looked on helplessly.

Fox was still working with the life jackets and making sure that the men were orderly and did not panic as the situation grew worse. The rush of water and the second wave of explosions from the engine room prevented anyone from getting below deck to gather more life jackets. The line was dwindling, but still there were numerous men without a jacket and no way to get one. Knowing that there was nothing more to do for the ship, the captain sent all the crew up to the deck so they could attempt to get on a lifeboat before it went under.

The lifeboat situation was still difficult, but it had begun to improve. Growing accustomed to working with the ropes encased in ice, the crews were able to lower the second lifeboat to the water without any major problems. The lifeboat slowly eased away from the sinking ship.

"What are we going to do?" cried one fearful voice after another. The men still standing on deck had gathered in small crowds of about ten. Anxious and confused, they were not thinking clearly. Ice-cold water sloshed on them and the bitter wind froze it to their hair, coats, and faces. Some lifeboats were too damaged by the ice to be used at all, others were risky, and there were still many without life jackets.

Fox mingled through the small huddles of men, praying with them and attempting to calm their fears. As he walked through the crowd, his eyes landed on a young soldier he had spoken to in previous days. Slowly making his way over to the soldier, Fox met his fearful eyes and rested a hand on his shoulder.

"Where's your jacket?" Fox asked slowly.

"I left it down below," the young man whispered, tears filling his eyes even as he tried to blink them away. Nodding, Fox thought only for a second before silently reaching up and pulling his life jacket over his head, placing it in the hands of the young soldier.

Shaking his head in disbelief, the soldier attempted to give it back, but Fox refused. "Go with God," Fox whispered to the young soldier as he began to pray once again.

The three other chaplains, spread out over different parts of the boat, all felt the same pull on their hearts, and they, too, gave up their jackets to those in need. As the ship began to lurch downward, water sloshing over the deck, the four chaplains stood together, offering up prayers for the men in the lifeboats and those not yet able to catch one.

Overwhelmed by desperation, some men leaped into the water. Others attempted to get the lifeboats in some working order, and still others joined the chaplains in prayer, knowing that the next few moments would likely be their last.

The ship did not take long to sink. In fact, the whole process took approximately a half-hour from the time they were hit. In the final moments prayers of praise and hope echoed out across the water, reaching the men in the ocean and those who had managed to remain in a lifeboat. The picture of the four chaplains standing together and singing praises to God as they sacrificed their lives for others is said to be burned in the memory of all who survived that night. The heroism and Christian faith in action that Fox and the other chaplains modeled that night touched not only the men who survived due to the life jackets, but others who witnessed or were later told of the event. Soldiers whose hearts had been hard came to know the Lord that very night. Sitting in the freezing boats in the dark, traumatic night, they found peace with God.

The next morning approximately 245 out of the 902 passengers were still alive. Rescue boats rushed them to immediate medical treatment, but in the end only 230 passengers survived. It was a tragic night, and yet even in such tragedy God's presence was clearly felt in the spirits of the men.

Operation Thunderbolt went on as soon as other men arrived in Greenland as reinforcements. The survivors worked with an intensity that impressed everyone who saw them. They knew they were blessed to be alive, and they possessed a renewed purpose and interest in living for a reason. Many found that reason in Christ, and revival entered their hearts and minds.

George Fox loved his country, but even more than that, Fox loved his Lord. This was evident not only in the great sacrifice that ended his life, but also in the daily living that brought him to that point. Although he was greatly missed by those he left behind, he left with them a legacy that will carry on forever.

ROBERT PRESTON TAYLOR

one

Robert Preston Taylor's early life prepared him for the difficult road ahead by supplying him with the love, faith, and experiences necessary to teach him how to live for the Lord. He spent his youth within the loving arms of a close-knit family life. The son of William Louis Taylor, he grew up in East Texas with his six brothers. His mother was a vital influence on his life and sought to raise her children in a way that honored the Lord.

The Taylors owned a nursery for part of Robert's childhood; later they purchased a ranch between Kilgore and Gladewater. The lifestyle of the ranch was vastly different from that of their previous home, but the boys adjusted quickly to their new surroundings. The plowing, hunting, and maintenance of the ranch kept them busy. Still, there were bright, sunny afternoons that could be spent with friends swimming in the creek or fishing at a favored spot. Such activities were treats for the growing boys, who were learning the value of both hard work and relaxation.

One of those summer days, Taylor found himself at a revival meeting. They were fairly common at the time, and perhaps he had attended them before, but that year something struck him. He heard the message the Methodist preacher presented and began to feel a stirring in his heart. He spoke with the preacher afterward but was not yet ready to commit himself to the Lord. The revival meeting drew to a close without Taylor making a commitment, but he thought long and hard about all he had heard.

The following summer brought Taylor's fifteenth birthday and another set of revival meetings. The preacher's words had dwelled in his mind all year, and he arrived at the revivals ready to learn and become a Christian. After the preacher shared with the crowd, an invitation was made for those who wanted to come forward and make a commitment to God.

Taylor sat for only a moment before standing on suddenly weak legs and making his way down to the front of the crowd. Amid his family and the fellowship of all in attendance, Taylor made the life-altering commitment to serve the Lord with his whole heart. His mother joined him at the altar, praying with her son and shedding tears of joy for his commitment. Taylor felt a deep personal change in himself, as if in that moment he had gained a clarity never before experienced in his life. He found peace deep within, knowing that God's perfect forgiveness was upon him.

Taylor left the revival looking no different on the outside, but everything had changed on the inside. He looked at the world with new eyes, longing to come to a greater understanding of God's character and actions. He was startled and yet somehow not surprised when the preacher placed a hand on his shoulder and said to him, "Someday the Lord may call you to preach, to share His Word with the world, and you'll do a fine job through His power." Taylor met the man's eyes, unsure how to respond, but the thought of preaching stayed with him.

Taylor returned home and the revival meetings closed again, but his commitment remained in his heart. He faithfully attended church services, reading his Bible regularly and always desiring a greater understanding of God. He shared with his friends how God was working in his heart, and words just seemed to flow from his mouth whenever God was brought up in conversation. He was soon invited to begin teaching Sunday school classes at his church. Many of the older women began to pray and speculate on Taylor's future as a preacher.

The months that followed were busy. He worked hard at his chores, helping his family as much as he possibly could. He also spent hours reading the Bible and becoming familiar with the great Christian leaders of the past. He saw not only their stories, but how their lives related to his life. He loved to read the words and spent as much time as he could absorbing the biblical truths he was discovering.

Something was becoming increasingly clear in the depths of Taylor's heart: His mission in life would be in full-time ministry. He knew he would never be able to settle for anything else.

Others also recognized his call. His parents watched the transformation in his life, seeing within him a fire for the Lord, and they knew that it was meant to be used in a powerful way.

Two years before his high-school education was complete, Taylor's mother called him into the kitchen for a talk.

"Your father and I have thought about this a lot. We have prayed for the Lord's guidance, and we have come to a conclusion," she said. Taylor sat in silent anticipation, unsure what his mother would say next.

"If preaching is what you are going to do with your life, then you should finish your schooling at the Baptist Academy in Jacksonville."

Taylor sat still, thinking through what his mother had just said. They would send him to school so he could begin his training in ministry, which was his dream. This would involve some struggles, of course. He would have to leave behind his family, friends, and church. "Lord, show me the way," he silently prayed, seeking to know the next step.

As he sat at the table, he realized he was asking the Lord for answers he already had. In moments it was completely settled in his mind. He knew the Lord was calling him to this, and no matter how difficult it would be to go forth on this journey, he knew it was the path the Lord had for him. "I'll go," he said softly.

Taylor worked hard through the remainder of high school, coming home in the summers to work on the ranch before returning to his schooling. He grew tremendously during that time, soaking up the knowledge of God and learning how to share it with others. From the Baptist Academy, he went on to Jacksonville Junior College. His time there was full of activities, and he began preaching too regularly to return home for work on the ranch. His family was incredibly proud of all he was doing. They were delighted when he could come to visit but did not expect him to return for work.

When the Great Depression set in, many young men dropped out of school to help their families. The ranch, however, was holding its own, and the family was able to pull together enough money to help support Taylor on his next leg of schooling. Baylor University, which possessed the best Bible department in the southwest, accepted Taylor straight from junior college. He was delighted, not only because of the impressive stature of their programs, but because they gave scholarships to young preachers.

Taylor attended both seminary and graduate school.

He was already an acclaimed speaker known for his open heart, never exalting himself above his congregation but working beside it, leading it to a greater understanding of God through day-to-day life.

While in graduate school, Taylor met his future wife, Ione, a kind, gentle, and very beautiful young woman. The day she agreed to marry him was the happiest day of his young life. They married soon after and began to build a life together. She was there for him as he began his early ministry, always attending his services and offering him her encouraging smile. A well-liked woman, she led the women of the church in a quiet but committed way. Their ministry together was a great blessing to others and to their marriage.

By 1938, Taylor's reputation had spread throughout Texas. He was known for his heart for the Lord and his skills in public speaking. A true pulpiteer, he delivered sermons that inspired and enriched the hearts of the congregation. He also sought to be personally involved in the lives of those in his pastoral care.

His early ministry days were spent at Hickory Grove Baptist Church, but in 1938 he was offered a position at South Fort Worth Baptist Church. The new church would be a challenge; it was bigger and demanded a greater amount of time and commitment. Taylor prayed carefully over the decision and knew the Lord was leading him into this exciting new opportunity.

One such new opportunity came as a complete surprise to Taylor. In the spring of 1938 he received a letter that requested he spend parts of the summer ministering to the troops in the camps. The letter was from the Chaplain's Division of the War Department, which was short on chaplains because of the recent buildup of troops. Taylor had not realized that many soldiers were without spiritual guidance and felt immediately burdened to serve them. He accepted a commission in the reserve and spent much of the summer working with troops at Fort Hood, just outside San Antonio.

"Men, always go into battle armed not only with the ammunition needed to stand against your enemy, but with the spiritual guidance of the Lord. You will need that if you are to ever truly stand at all," he instructed the young men. Taylor left Fort Hood at the end of summer to return to his church and ministry, but he did not forget the men or their needs.

A second call from the Chaplain's Division of the War Department came in 1940. This time they requested that he spend a year with troops. The exact location was not revealed, but he knew he would be somewhere in the Orient. This decision was very difficult for him. He felt a burden to answer the call and help the soldiers, but he also had a church he was responsible for at home. He would also have to leave his wife alone for a full year. The thought was heartbreaking and drove him to his knees in prayer for many days. At the end of that time, he knew the Lord was calling him to the Orient. After discussing it with

Ione and the leaders in the church, he formally agreed to go and minister to the soldiers.

Good-byes were difficult and tearful. Ione was the only one who came with him that morning, sending him off with her love and prayers for a safe return. The members of the church had also offered their prayer support, encouraging their pastor and letting him know that they supported his decision.

two

Taylor traveled on the USAT *Washington,* sailing into Manila Bay, the Philippines, where he would be stationed. He was assigned to the 31st Infantry, which possessed a proud military history and was the only full American regiment in the Philippines. They were quartered in the center of the city, in the heart of the action within the historic walls of Manila.

There were many adjustments for Taylor in those first few days. He was taken to his quarters, where he began to meet others, but loneliness was heavy on his heart. Then he began to find his footing in his work. The Lord gave him a vision of how he could best serve the soldiers, and Taylor began to look for ways to live that. He knew he needed two things: to get to know the soldiers and to have large worship services where the gospel could be preached to all who would listen. Those two early goals of his ministry came together much more quickly than he would have imagined possible.

There were two services on Sundays, both of which were going very well, but Taylor felt there was something missing. He scheduled a prayer meeting for Wednesday nights, which was held in the theater inside Cuartel de Espana. Following the prayer meeting was a mid-week movie. Taylor was never quite sure which was attracting the people, the prayer meeting or the movie.

There was soon a new burden on Taylor's heart, even though his current ministry activities continued to grow. The city offered a massive amount of sinister distractions, and many young soldiers attempted to drown their loneliness at the bars and nightclubs. Taylor knew such distractions were not going to help the troops in the long run. He wanted to find ways to help the young men keep from falling prey to such temptations.

The B Range was a quarantine section for arriving soldiers. They were kept there for a time, training apart from everyone else, so if they brought diseases with them, they would not spread to the city. The young men were confined to the base when they arrived. Taylor felt that time of isolation was when he would have the most success reaching the young men for the Lord. After a Wednesday night prayer meeting, he brought the idea up to Chaplain Dawson.

Chaplain William Dawson, who had been Taylor's closest friend in seminary, had recently returned to Manila and was working alongside Taylor. They began splitting the preaching at the services and prayerfully supporting each other in their times of need.

"I've been thinking about the men arriving on B Range," Taylor said one night after the service. "They need the gospel message before they are overwhelmed with the temptations of this city."

"I agree; they need to find the peace they're looking for in God," Dawson responded as his mind thought through the possibilities.

"We know they are not going to find what they are looking for in the bars of the city," Taylor continued. The two chaplains went to the Lord in prayer, asking for open doors and ready hearts so the message they shared would be well received. They also asked for wisdom in how to best approach beginning ministries in an area that would be new to them both.

It did not take long for Taylor to realize how ready the young soldiers at B Range really were. He visited there a few days before he planned on beginning services, in hopes of getting to know some of the men. He spent the days getting acquainted with the troops, teasing them and encouraging them as they all grew comfortable with one another.

The young men quickly began to see Taylor as a friend and mentor, someone willing to help them through the difficult transition they faced. They teased him mercilessly on many occasions, but they also sought him out whenever the loneliness or fear was overwhelming. They knew they could talk to him openly and he would support them however he could.

The first Sunday after his arrival, Taylor set up a tent in the middle of the camp and began announcing morning service. He was overwhelmed by the response and delighted at the number of enthusiastic men who came. His message that first day was "The Tragedy of Sin," something that had burdened his heart since he began praying for the men. All had spent time with the chaplain; he had earned their respect, and they were eager to hear what he would share.

Taylor spoke of the roots of sin, how it seeps into a man's life and eats away at it until his personal life is in shambles. He also shared the salvation and relief found in the person of Jesus Christ. His words resounded throughout the camp, and many of the men felt themselves coming to a better understanding of who they wanted to become. Taylor's final charge to the young men was one of encouragement. He challenged them to not only be good soldiers for their country, but to be good soldiers for their Lord. As they sang the closing song, Taylor looked around the crowd and saw that many men appeared to be genuinely touched by his message.

In the days that followed, Taylor spent as much time with the young men as possible. He helped them put together messages for their families back home and arranged for them to be sent. He also met with men who had questions or concerns they needed to share. The men related to Taylor and fully accepted him into their lives. Although he still missed his family and congregation at home, he rejoiced that the Lord had called him to work with these men. The men rejoiced that "Chappie" was there for them as they adjusted to the struggles of soldiering and sought to understand more about life as a Christian.

three

At 4:30 A.M. on December 8, 1941, Captain Short ran into the room, shouting, "The Harbor was hit! War is starting! You've got to wake up!" Short quickly bounded out of the room to alert other officers of the situation.

Taylor walked through the early morning fog to report to Colonel Doane. By the time he arrived, a number of other officers were assembled and awaiting a briefing. All were anxious to know what was going to happen.

"We have Japs on their way to Manila. We'll need to prepare full field gear and set up in the valley south of McKinley." The colonel gave his orders, explaining the situation as briefly as possible before dismissing the men to prepare for the coming days. Taylor returned to his quarters to briskly pack his bags. The radio was announcing the details of the Pearl Harbor attack, but Taylor did not listen for long. He paused to pray and hurried on with his day.

The city was calm and quiet as he walked on. People had not yet begun to comprehend the seriousness of what was taking place. As Taylor walked through the streets toward his destination, he heard the shrill sound of sirens pierce the quiet air. The sirens signaled air raids, which began approximately at 11:30 A.M.

Traffic halted and people scattered, everyone searching for a place to hide and shelter the children. At first Taylor saw the planes were circling and attacking only the military areas. He hoped the city itself would be spared but soon realized that would not be the case. He counted twenty-seven bombers in place, and fire was spreading rapidly around the city.

The destruction of the city was horrible. Taylor watched people rushing about in an effort to salvage whatever they could. Firemen struggled to contain the blazes, only to find that their hoses had been cut by Japanese sympathizers. The fire trucks would not have been much help amid such destruction, but it was a blow to the city that they were completely out of commission in such a time of need. The attacks continued, destroying the harbor and bringing havoc throughout the once beautiful and historic city.

Taylor rushed to help the injured. He was able to use his jeep to transport many to the hospital between attacks. He looked around the city with a profound sense of sorrow. The beautiful city was now a heap of rubble; the stench of fire and death hung in the air; and everywhere he looked, he saw hurting, frightened people. One little boy sat quietly across from the Santo Domingo Cathedral, which was burning down. Taylor said nothing, weeping quietly alongside the young child, overcome by the horrors unfolding before his very eyes. As he sat and wept, Taylor heard bells chiming across the city in one loud accord, mourning the loss and yet proclaiming victory in Christ.

Those church bells were a turning point in Taylor's life. He knew that there was nothing he could do about the destruction around him. He was powerless against the force of war, which would touch both civilian and military alike. He was not powerless, though, in his ministry to the soldiers who would be dealing with the devastation and its consequences. He committed his heart to serving the Lord wholeheartedly in the war, reaching the men and ministering to them as they dealt with what would likely be the greatest trial of their lives.

A short while later, Taylor reached camp in the small valley just south of Fort William McKinley. The mood of the camp was subdued. Small clusters of whispering soldiers stood together in anticipation. Taylor knew that this moment was pivotal, not only for himself, but for all the men at the camp, who would be fearful and seeking difficult answers. He announced that a worship service would begin at 1900 hours and immediately went about preparing for it.

The service was full; the men crowded together, anxious to hear their chaplain speak. Taylor shared with them encouragement from the gospel, Christ's promise never to leave His people alone. He told them of the ever-present power of the Lord and assured them that they would never enter battle alone.

At the close of the service, the regiment's assignment was announced: guarding the city of Bataan. This was difficult news to hear, for Bataan was known for the disease-infested jungle areas that surrounded it. Bataan was often termed a hardship post. The men left the service clinging to the words of Christ and the sermon that Taylor preached. They knew they faced difficult days ahead.

As the men cleared out, Colonel Doane stayed behind to speak to the chaplain alone. "Don't ever think that what you are doing here isn't important," the colonel warned Taylor. "It is perhaps the most important thing, because you are impacting their lives and their hearts forever. Things will get rough in the coming weeks, but I know you'll be all right. Pray. Read the Word. Share it all with the men. It will be enough, and it will be what carries us through."

Taylor stood for a moment in silent contemplation of all the colonel was saying. He felt the fear around his heart—the insecurity that perhaps he was not up for the job—begin to melt away. He was not up for the job, but God was. "Thank you, Colonel," Taylor responded. The colonel nodded before moving onto details they needed to discuss.

He would supply Taylor with a jeep and an assistant so that he would have complete access to the troops wherever there was a need. Taylor knew that was a true blessing, for there was a very limited number of vehicles.

Three days later, the 31st broke camp and headed for Bataan. Taylor left the security of the fort and ventured forth on the mission, unsure of what was ahead but trusting the Lord to lead the way.

four

The men arrived outside the town of Bataan with orders to maintain the security of the two main roads. The roads were known as East and West. Running along the coast, they would be pivotal in the looming battles. Soldiers got quickly to work, setting up trenches and foxholes. They also set barbed wire around the areas for extra protection. The men were confident that with the shelter of the jungle and the preparedness of their trenches, they could maintain control of the roads. The wild card in all of that would be the logistical support needed in order for the platoons to know their next moves.

December 10, 1941, the Japanese started their ground offensive in neighboring areas and cities. They did not push through with a major thrust at first, so men waiting in the trenches did not see battle that first week. That gave them a lot of spare time to think and worry about what was ahead.

"This waiting isn't helping the men. They need to talk more, think less, and stop anticipating the next move so much," Taylor observed. He sensed the restlessness and nerves within the groups of men and decided he would do something to get their minds in a healthier place.

Still having the jeep, Taylor moved from one group to the next throughout the day. He was greeted with cheers and laughter—a welcome relief to the monotony that had become their days. Sitting down with them in their foxholes, he joined in the conversation. If the opportunity arose, he would share with them from the Bible, pray with them, and encourage them to trust the Lord in confusing times.

That became Taylor's routine. He spent his days moving from one platoon to the next, sharing with the men and seeking to relieve their stress. It brought a new sense of peace to Taylor's heart, too, and he was encouraged by the improving morale of the men.

Tense days gave way to more tense days while the men awaited the Japanese move. Eventually the waiting was over. Early one dawn, a major invasion hit the area. The Japanese soldiers totaled eighty thousand men. Taylor's units were given orders to relocate, to better maintain the city. Marching with the soldiers, he was struck by how much he needed the Lord's power to sustain him under such difficult situations. He turned to prayer as he marched, looking to God for strength and wisdom for the coming trials and battles.

Christmas Eve arrived in the midst of preparations, the regiment still not having fully entered into battle. Taylor was momentarily struck by guilt when he forgot what day it was. Then he let go of the guilt and tried to find a way to hold Christmas services. Christmas morning dawned clear and brisk, and Taylor took advantage of the earliest rays of light to begin his rounds. This day the rounds were special because he would be sharing the Christmas story. Holidays spent away from family were always a difficult time for soldiers, but Taylor sought to make them understand the greater joy they could find only in Christ. Many men opened their hearts to the Lord that day; the Christmas spirit was alive among the soldiers, even in the heat of war.

A pattern of battle formed. The men would fight against a sizable force, then retreat, dynamiting bridges and holding the Japanese soldiers from further advances. It worked well and kept the Japanese at bay, even in difficult battles.

Days passed quickly, and soon the Japanese combined troops to launch a massive attack against the 31st. The troops were prepared, but the devastation of battle was soon among them. The American troops held their ground, tightly entrenched. They were able to fend off the advancing Japanese with machine-gun fire and blockades of barbed wire, but they knew a new attack would soon follow.

Taylor tended to the wounded, getting them to bunkers and collecting the dog tags of those who did not survive. The stench of death, caked blood, and gunfire filled the air and sickened him. He pushed forward, doing his best to be of service to the men. His first experience in full-fledged battle was grueling and horrible to witness. His stomach retched and his body trembled at the sight of his men in so much pain, the loss of life, and the knowledge that it would start all over again the next day.

The Japanese prepared for a major frontal assault against the American troops, dropping leaflets encouraging surrender as their planes flew overhead. Surrender was not an option. The troops prepared to face the Japanese army head-on.

"I can't eat; the stench is so bad. I can't sleep for fear of what will happen next. And I can't stand still 'cause I've got too much energy to just think," a young soldier confided in Taylor as he made his rounds.

The tropical sun intensified the stench of blood that hung in the air, making most men lose their appetite, and the fear of what would happen next in battle loomed over their heads like a storm cloud.

"Son, I know these are difficult times, and I haven't been able to eat much, either, but the best thing you can do is just focus on the little things. Take care of yourself, look out for the men around you, and keep focused on what you're doing. The Bible tells us not to borrow tomorrow's troubles because today has enough trouble of its own. Hold onto that. Just focus on today and trust God for tomorrow."

"It's so difficult not to think about what's going to happen," the young man said sadly.

"I know, and I think about it, too, but in those times when you start thinking too much, start praying. Ask God to help you get through this, ask Him to give you the wisdom and the courage to face what tomorrow will bring, and then get back to focusing on what you can do today." Taylor paused, meeting the man's eyes and allowing him the time to think about what he had said.

"Will you pray with me, Chaplain?" he asked quietly.

"I'd be honored," Taylor responded before turning to prayer for the young soldier and all those he fought alongside.

Taylor was soon assigned to Graves Registration burial detail. He worked hard for the men, knowing they had died honorable deaths in battle and wanting to give them the best possible care. It was a difficult job, though, and it pounded hard on his heart to see the massive casualties the continuous battle was beginning to yield. The Japanese bombers continued their assaults along the American lines, and though the Americans held strong, it became increasingly difficult to maintain their defense.

Taylor went down the line, picking up the dead and using the time for ministry. He encouraged the men and took the time to pray with them before moving along to the next area. It became increasingly clear that morale was very low and the loss of life was wearing on the soldiers. They watched horrors day after day, wondering what would happen next, and it soon became apparent that there was a limit to what even the most courageous of men could endure.

The assaults by the Japanese were not the most damaging situation the American troops were facing. The disease-infested jungle overflowed with illnesses that spread quickly through the troops. Food was scarce, and rations were cut by 50 percent, leaving the men hungry and without proper nutrition to maintain their health. They had no way to obtain more food, and once the horse and mule meat was eaten, they resorted to hunting monkeys and cobras. Malaria spread quickly through the hungry, tired troops, and soon both hospitals overflowed with more patients than they could handle. The disease-trodden, emaciated troops struggled to maintain control as the situation worsened and the death toll continued to increase.

At the hospitals, supplies quickly became scarce. Hundreds of men arrived in the early stages of malaria, but with the last of the medicine already distributed, the doctor found there was virtually nothing he could do. The men were tended to with the best possible care, but without the proper medications, the death rate was very high. It became increasingly clear to Taylor that at the rate things were going, soon the ammunition and rations would be all but completely gone. Things were not looking good, but isolated troops held the Japanese off, even while they suffered immensely for it.

As the battle grew worse, the colonel saw there was only one option left. Two-thirds of his forces were sick, others were injured, and five thousand new Japanese soldiers were being brought in for battle. All the odds were stacked against the Americans. A full retreat was ordered. Across the island, soldiers began to fall back. They were told to destroy any weapons they could not take with them. As difficult as it was to destroy their greatest protection, the men set to work disarming weapons and vehicles.

By that point, every other front had been captured by the Japanese. It was a sorrowful time as the troops fell back, but the colonel was proud of his men and all they had done to defend their positions. Many had arrived with virtually no training; others came from different branches of the service; still they pulled together and would have willingly given their lives to hold strong in their positions. Even as they fell back, offering counterattacks as the Japanese continued their onslaught, the men fought hard and diligently through night and day.

Now that all other areas were under Japanese control, the 31st fell under the full force of the Japanese bombardment. They were attacked on land and from the sky, and Taylor quickly realized that surrender was becoming their only option. Still, they pushed forward.

Easter Sunday was a troublesome day for the troops,

who still maintained their new positions and endured the heavy brunt of the Japanese army. Taylor spent the morning and early afternoon moving around small groups of men, sharing from the Bible, and praying with them. He saw many reach for their own pocket New Testaments and was encouraged that they were turning to the Lord. He prayed their commitments to the Lord would carry them through the difficult days ahead. He prayed also for those who resisted the message, for they were lost in a horrible time with no one to turn to for guidance.

The turning point of the battle arrived on March 7, when the 31st could no longer endure the heavy assault. The defeated army struggled through the jungle, retreating as quickly as possible amid the fatigue and sickness that plagued them all. Taylor worked with the first-aid areas, supplying the men with hot coffee and soup as they reached Limay Valley.

Taylor helped keep the men's morale up as much as he could, but they all knew what waited in the distance: surrender. It was now only a matter of time before the men would be forced to surrender, and fear of the capitulation outweighed even the greatest fears of battle. Unable to sleep amid such need, Taylor worked day and night serving the men through the first-aid area and by moving from group to group for prayer and Bible study.

"We've got to get these men, the most seriously injured, out of here, or they will never make it," the doctor told Taylor one morning. The question was how they would transport sixty-five injured men to Baguio for treatment. Rounding up a broken-down bus, Taylor and his assistant managed to get it in good enough condition to make the trip. It would not be the ideal way to transport the injured, but it would likely save their lives.

The job was swiftly completed. Upon delivery of the men, they were ordered to destroy the buses so they would not fall into Japanese hands. Before they had the chance to do so, the doctors asked that the chaplain deliver twenty nurses to a boat that awaited them at Mariveles. Taylor escorted the nurses onto the bus and sought to bring a measure of comfort to them. Evidence of the Japanese bombings and land attacks were everywhere along the road, and the ladies looked nervously on, in fear of what would happen to them if captured.

It was a difficult trip for Taylor, not simply because of the risk of Japanese assaults, but because of a message he had to deliver.

"May I speak to Nurse Helen Summers, please?" Taylor inquired of a woman seated at the front of the bus. After being directed to the correct nurse, Taylor sat down and introduced himself.

"How can I help you, Chaplain?" the pretty young nurse inquired.

"I'm sorry to say that I have some bad news for you," Taylor solemnly informed her. "Arnold Benjamin was killed just days ago in the battle for Mount Sumat."

Helen sat in shocked silence for a moment. "But we're going to be married," she whispered.

"I'm so sorry," Taylor told her as the news began to sink in. Death had become a regular part of life in the Philippines, but when it struck so close to home, it hit a whole new level. Taylor spoke briefly with Nurse Summers, telling her of the heroism Benjamin had displayed, but he soon left her to her thoughts, knowing it would take time to deal with such a loss.

The buses arrived safely at the harbor and the nurses were carried off the peninsula. Once they were out of sight and clearly in friendly waters, Taylor and the other men prepared to rejoin their group and await the surrender that was sure to come. The bugles were silent, the men contemplative, and the air full of tension as the hours passed and the growing sense of fear increased.

Taylor held one last group prayer service with his men, encouraging them to trust in the Lord no matter what was ahead. Soon after, the surrender was official, and the Japanese were in control.

five

Answering a general order sent out to all remaining troops, the men raised the white flag at 10:00 A.M. amid mixed emotions. Not long after that the Japanese, advancing slowly for fear of any final resistance, came upon the troops. They harshly tore down the American flag, shredded it, and stomped on it in a final gesture of triumph. The Japanese officers then took control of the hospital and ordered all soldiers to gather in front of the main entrance.

The men gathered, nervously trying to protect the wounded as they awaited Japanese orders. The Japanese soldiers made short work of stripping the soldiers of all watches, rings, and personal belongings. With a final look of regret, Taylor gave up his wedding band and university ring. It was a dehumanizing moment for many of the soldiers, but it was nothing compared to what was yet to come.

As the day progressed, a sense of serenity was once again restored to the jungle. Guns no longer fired, smoke and dust began to clear, and animals were again moving about. It was a false sense of calm, though, because it brought with it even greater dangers.

"We did our job. No matter what it cost us, we did our job." Soldiers whispered that sentiment throughout the day. Surrender was not an easy thing for them to do, but they did it with the knowledge that they had served a purpose. They had held the line so well that the Japanese had to send in troops from other locations, which halted the Japanese assault in many other areas, especially Australia. They gave themselves up amid disease and starvation, but they had served their country well as what was later termed a "sacrificial holding force."

Late in the evening an interpreter approached, letting all the men know that they would be moving to Mariveles. The doctors could remain to tend to the patients unable to move, but the rest would be marching out that night. Taylor joined the line of men walking the east road, where they were picked up in trucks and taken to Mariveles.

The Japanese officials were faced with a growing crisis. They had anticipated the capture of approximately twenty thousand prisoners, but instead they had captured close to eighty thousand. There were also complications involving the Filipino citizens who were fleeing the cities. The guards tried to arrange the men into groups of three hundred. It was a miserable failure and greatly frustrating situation, as the men milled around in groups of thousands. The Japanese soldiers, growing more frustrated with every passing moment, shouted out orders in Japanese. The prisoners, who did not understand the orders anyway, were kicked, slapped, and otherwise abused when the orders were not followed. It was a troubling situation to watch and a horrible situation to be in the center of.

Taylor learned quickly that there was nothing he could do but pray. Anything else was greeted by the officials with abuse to him and to any men he attempted to assist. At night all had to remain completely silent. Even the slightest noise—coughing, crackling leaves, or movement—would bring rounds of artillery fire.

Not that the noise mattered much. Throughout the night there were sporadic bursts of machine-gun fire without purpose. The fire would be followed by screams, then silence would once again reign until the pattern was repeated. The captured soldiers spent their night in fear, wondering what the new day would bring.

By noon the next day the men had not been given food or water in over twenty-four hours. Heat exhaustion and lingering illnesses from the weeks of battle took a toll on them all. Many men began to fall, unable to stand any longer. Their buddies attempted to pick them up quickly, because anyone who could not stand was bayoneted.

The Japanese soldiers viewed themselves as patriots freeing their homelands from the American imperialistic government that had tried to take them. It was a distorted image that drove them forward and compelled them to acts of violence without provocation. Taylor soon realized that the Japanese soldiers would not be honoring any world agreements on the proper treatment of POWs. Instead, they were doing whatever they chose. The POWs were a hassle, and the Japanese officials saw no reason to treat them humanely when they viewed America in such a negative and vindictive light. At 1:00 P.M. the soldiers were given marching orders, told to carry what they could and move along with the guards. Still without food and water, the soldiers had no choice but to move forward in a long line, with no real understanding of where they were going. Guards stood approximately twenty feet apart, making sure that the men stayed on task and entertaining themselves by harassing their weary, downtrodden prisoners.

Taylor had previously met Chaplain Father Duffy, a committed man deep in faith and possessing a great amount of love. They fell in line close to each other, unable to speak but comforted by one another's presence. A guard noticed a cross around Father Duffy's neck and, bringing his bayonet against Father Duffy's chest, proceeded to rip the cross off and fling it to the dirt.

Through the coming days Father Duffy jokingly termed the guard "the Shadow" because he seemed to arrive everywhere Duffy marched and harassed him any time he got the chance. Taylor began marching directly behind Duffy, because each time Duffy slowed or lagged behind, the Shadow would hit him with the butt of his rifle. Soon Duffy's face was caked with blood. Taylor often stepped ahead for a moment, placing his arm around Duffey's shoulders and giving him a brief moment of rest. It was not much, but it was the best he could do for his weary friend.

Taylor himself was weary and burdened, fatigued and thirsty. He distracted himself by going over seminary lessons, reciting verses in his mind, or listing attributes of God. All this reminded him who was really in control, a difficult lesson when the Japanese soldiers were inflicting pain upon them all.

There was a soldier Taylor knew who went by the name of Tex. No one really knew where the nickname had started, because the man hailed from Nevada, but Tex was what everyone called him. Taylor marched alongside Tex, growing increasingly concerned for his health with every passing moment. He had been suffering from dysentery for days and was often delirious. Taylor attempted to keep him lucid by talking to him, but often Tex would stare into space at nothing in particular.

About two hours into the march, Tex dropped his bundle and fell into the dust, unable to move another step. Taylor heard the approaching guards and quickly placed himself between them and Tex. Another soldier and Taylor got Tex up and moving again, but Tex was in absolute agony. In desperation, Taylor called out to the guards, begging them for just a little bit of water or medicine.

The guards ordered Taylor back into line. *Korosuzo!* they shouted, threatening to kill him if he did not comply. Other soldiers stepped forward and pulled Taylor back into place. After a few steps he heard gasps and cries. He turned to see Tex's body pushed to the side of the road as a Japanese soldier cleaned blood from his bayonet.

At that moment Taylor realized the depth of pain they were going to endure and the number of lives that would be lost because of it. He continued marching, too weary to think clearly about the loss of such a young and vibrant man and knowing that he was far from the first casualty of the day. He would also not be the last.

The road was steep and treacherous, causing men to stumble and fall at every turn. The guards were right there, and the fallen men were quickly eliminated.

At one point Taylor witnessed a guard push two prisoners over the side of a cliff strictly for amusement. They had not done anything to anger the guard and were standing with their hands silently lifted in supplication. Their screams rang out across the lines until they faded on the jagged rocks below.

The marching continued with no rest. Taylor glanced ahead and saw literally miles of men marching ahead of him, guards lining the road waiting for them to fall. The march was quickly turning into a blood-bath. Something needed to be done, but there were no options for the troops, who had to march onward or face execution.

At one point the guards called out for greater speed, rushing the troops along at a speed many could not handle. It had been far too long since they had food or water, and their bodies were giving out. Many men dropped. They were automatically bayoneted, and those who attempted to help were shot. Many were seeing mirages; others, unable to cope anymore, fell willingly into the grips of death.

One such man, a veteran of World War I, could not move another step. Delirious and on the brink of death, he stopped and opened his shirt, begging for someone to end his pain. The guards would not allow his death to come easily. They pulled a young boy from the crowd, which consisted not only of soldiers but also captured Filipino women and children. The young boy was held at gunpoint and instructed to beat the older man with a club. Trembling and biting back tears, the boy raised the club and, with his eyes closed, struck the man, who fell to the ground in death. The boy, traumatized by the event and everything that surrounded the march, lost his mind and never recovered. In many ways his life was ended that day, as well.

Taylor soon began to feel the full force of thirst. He was tormented with images of water, longing for it at every turn. Walking along practically in a trace, his mind would run in and out of coherency. His thoughts all began to center on his need for refreshment. Leg cramps and blistery sunburn tore at him. With the lack of water and food, he was not sure how he could take another step. Taylor turned his heart to God as much as he could and continued walking slowly up the mountain, following the ever-dwindling line of POWs.

Early the following morning, the men reached the top of the mountain. Relieved to have the march up the winding road completed, the weary men knew a moment of peace—only a moment. The townspeople came out to hand them food and water. Father Duffy was one of those handed a cup of water. The Shadow had other ideas. Using the butt of his rifle, he slammed Father Duffy in the mouth, sending the water flying, along with fresh blood. Dropping to his knees, unable to stand a moment longer, Father Duffy prayed for the Lord's presence to be known in his life. The guard, infuriated by the response, drove his bayonet into Father Duffy's side and kicked him to the ground.

Taylor rushed to his friend's side, kneeling over him in an effort to block further attacks. It was too late to do anything for his friend. Saying a silent prayer, he allowed the other soldiers to pull him away and watched as villagers moved Father Duffy's body off the road.

"I can't believe this," Taylor whispered softly as he marched onward, still caught in the haze of dehydration.

"A friend of yours?" another soldier asked, nodding

his head toward Father Duffy.

"A great friend and a great man," Taylor acknowledged as the guards yelled for silence in the lines.

Miraculously, Father Duffy would survive the brutal bayonet attack and later be reunited with Taylor. But that joyful moment would come after much more turmoil and pain.

Turning their thoughts inward once again, the men attempted to keep their minds from falling prey to the hysteria that swirled around them.

Taylor felt his mind wandering. He experienced complete blackouts when the sun and lack of water affected his mind. He came up with as many little tricks as he could think of to keep his mind occupied and coherent. He counted the days of the week, month, and year, then repeated them backwards. He thought of his family, describing each of them and trying to remember important dates in their lives. He thought of his wife, Ione, and wondered what she was doing. Was she thinking of him? Had someone told her he was captured? Would she think he was dead? He tried to pray for them all. Sometimes he would remain alert enough to do so; other times his mind could not handle the task.

It was not just the lack of water and the heat of the sun that was tearing at Taylor's mind. He was continually witnessing the cruel deaths of those he had served alongside in battle. He saw children killed without mercy. Men's lives were used as entertainment for the weary guards. The bodies lay along the road as constant reminders, and the stench of death was unmistakable. How could he reconcile the circumstance he was in with a God he knew was full of love? How did he forgive the men who were putting them through this horror? What he was seeing was too intense to comprehend, and he wondered if he would ever heal emotionally, assuming he lived that long.

Soon they passed through another small village. The Japanese had planned on parading the POWs through as a show of power but were greatly angered when the crowds cheered for the POWs and welcomed them. Many in the crowd brought food out and began throwing it at the starving prisoners. The Japanese attempted to keep the crowds back, but they continued to cheer and throw out more food.

Taylor caught a piece of hardened sugar cane and immediately began to suck on the sweet stick. It was the first food or drink he had had in three days, and although it wasn't much, it would keep him alive for now. After a moment, he broke the piece in half and handed it to Major Shurtz, who had been walking with Taylor since the loss of Father Duffy. Together Shurtz and Taylor made a pact to keep each other from going crazy and physically restrain each other if necessary. Many men, mad with thirst, were killed by guards in their search for water that did not exist. Others found little scummy puddles of water and drank thirstily, no longer caring what was living in there. Taylor and Shurtz did not want to fall prey to either end, so they agreed to guide each other through the trip the best they could.

After passing through the village, the POWs were corralled for the night and sent to sleep with no food or water. The following morning the guards made an attempt to feed their prisoners. Each POW was rationed three tablespoons of rice mush, but the guards threw it at the prisoners, and most of it ended up in the sand. Hoards of men were on their hands and knees clawing at the sand in hopes of getting even the slightest bit of nourishment. Satisfied with their attempts, the Japanese guards quickly hurried the prisoners back to marching.

six

The marching order was delayed. The large number of POWs and the length of the marching line often led to confusion among the guards, and this was one such time. The guards, frustrated and bored, decided to amuse themselves with a group of prisoners.

Taylor and Major Shurtz, along with eighteen other men, were pulled from the crowd and given a "sun treatment." Removing the men's shirts and shoes, the guards made them kneel with their faces turned up into the scorching sun. Heat exhaustion and delirium attacked Taylor's mind. He tried the old concentration games, but they were not enough to help, so he turned his mind to his seminary training, going over every assignment he had ever prepared in theology and preaching. He ran through the years, mentally reciting his oral exams and the presentations he gave to get his

196

doctorate. His mind remained focused, and even in the worst moments of his life thus far, he was able to think of God with love. As he was moving onto the final stages of thinking through his doctoral work, he felt a guard untying his hands.

He endured the torture for three hours, one among seven of the twenty to walk away alive. Shurtz had also survived, and the two moved silently back into the line of prisoners, too physically and emotionally worn to express what they had endured.

Taylor's mind deteriorated further. He saw colors running together in unfamiliar patterns when the heat played tricks on his eyes. He lived in a world of fantasy where he would have water, food, and shelter from the sun. He even began to focus on thoughts of death, which would bring relief, and escape, something to yearn for and welcome when it came. Then he would be out of his misery and in the Lord's hands.

In the midst of pondering his death, Taylor heard a voice calling to him. His instructions were clear: not death but life. It was not yet his time to meet death. Something stirred inside Taylor's mind and deep within his heart, and he began to cry out, "Alive! I'll live! I'll be alive!" Delirium mixed with inspiration sent him into a state of confusion, and when he came back to his senses he recognized Major Shurtz holding his shoulders and shaking him urgently. At that point a guard noticed the ruckus and came over to see what was happening. Taylor prepared himself for a beating or perhaps even death. Instead, the guard removed the canteen from his belt and handed it to Taylor. Confused, Taylor hesitated before slowly accepting the canteen and drinking thirstily. He passed the canteen to the major, who then passed it on along down the line. The guard walked away silently.

"Why would he do that?" Shurtz whispered in shock. "It makes no sense."

"Maybe he doesn't even know why he did it. Maybe it was Someone greater at work." Taylor did not know why the guard did what he did, but he did know that God used it to sustain him and give him hope. In those moments Taylor knew that he was going to live, that the Lord did indeed have a plan in mind, and that Taylor was part of that plan.

Soon after, the POWs arrived at Limay. They were put in a corral once used as a stable by Japanese cavalrymen. The guards again threw small portions of rice at the prisoners, but most of it again fell to the ground and mixed with the dirt. It appeared there would be no relief for their starving, dehydrated bodies.

"Look, ambulances!" Shurtz exclaimed as he pointed to the sight before them.

"I can't believe it," Taylor commented. The drivers were Japanese, but the lead vehicle contained an American officer—Colonel Schwartz, the hospital commander whom Taylor had worked closely with in the past.

Colonel Schwartz quickly looked over the prisoners.

Beaten and dirty, they were clearly lacking in all basic necessities for survival. He threw an angry frown at the Japanese guards and called for food and water to be brought immediately. The high-ranking Japanese officials nodded their permission, and adequate food and water was brought for the prisoners. Next the colonel called for the most dire emergencies to be brought forward to the ambulances so he could take them to the hospital. Taylor was helping a sickly man toward an ambulance when the colonel noticed him.

"Chaplain, is that really you?" Schwartz called out in shock. Taylor nodded, unable to communicate any further.

"You're coming with me," Schwartz commanded, knowing the hospital needed a chaplain and unable to watch Taylor suffer any further. Not that the hospital, now run by the Japanese, was much better, but it was all he could do.

"I hate to leave you," Taylor said, turning to Major Shurtz and the others around him. Taylor could find little peace about his personal relief when he knew how the others would be living.

"You've got to go," Shurtz said quietly. "God goes with you, and you'll be serving Him wherever you end up."

"God goes with you, as well. Remember that," Taylor told the major before turning and walking slowly toward the ambulance. Taylor knew that a prisoner named Bill had to go with him. He was in horrible shape and would never survive if left in the guards' hands. Taylor helped Bill up and carried him to the ambulances where Colonel Schwartz awaited. "He can't stay here any longer," Taylor explained.

"That's fine. Put him in the ambulance and hop in yourself. The men at the hospital need you." Taylor did as he was instructed, and within minutes found himself in the front seat with the colonel, leaving behind the gruesome reality he had barely survived.

"I bet you're wondering how this is possible—me having my freedom of movement and all," Schwartz said after a few moments on the road.

"It had crossed my mind," Taylor acknowledged, feeling much more alert now that he'd had food and water.

"During Bataan's battle, we took twenty-six wounded Japanese soldiers into the hospital. A Japanese general found out that the men received good medical treatment, so he allowed me to keep the hospital open. They even let me take the ambulances around to pick up the injured."

Taylor sat back, amazed at God's provision even in the worst of circumstances.

"We've got about three thousand patients there now, and I know anything you can do for them will be greatly appreciated," Schwartz continued.

"I'll do whatever I can," Taylor assured him, praising God for a light amid the darkness that had surrounded him for days.

seven

Taylor was able to spend a few days at the hospital. He showered, ate real meals, and tried to recover a sense of peace about all he had experienced. He struggled with the knowledge that he had survived while so many others were still suffering under the guards. Taylor knew that God had a purpose for everything, even when it was difficult to understand, so he did his best to work with the men in the hospital and leave the death march behind him.

The reprieve did not last long, because the hospital was located dangerously near a battleground and many casualties resulted. Taylor was once again in the midst of destruction, attempting to help as many as he could, even though the Japanese guards took the hospital and canceled the colonel's privileges. The men were transported to a holding area. Taylor once again found himself a full POW, thrust into Japanese hands and unable to defend himself.

He learned a great many things in the years that followed. He learned patience, endurance, and how to rely on God in the worst possible circumstances. He spent the next three and one-half years as a POW, often being transported on the hell-ships through different Japanese territories. He was gravely ill and severely abused. Everything he had ever known or loved was stripped from him—everything except the Lord. Through the darkest days of his life, through the anguish and the trials, Taylor remained true to his God and trusted that God was remaining true to him. As an example to many, a witness in words and deeds, God took the circumstances of Taylor's life—which men had meant for evil—and used them for good. It was not easy, and there were many times he would have accepted the relief of death, yet still Taylor pressed on.

At the end of his imprisonment, after he had struggled and suffered through years of abuse, neglect, and torture, Taylor was finally able to return home. It was a bittersweet homecoming, as his family had been informed of his death years before. His wife, Ione, had remarried. This was a devastating loss for Taylor, who had held out hope that someday he would be with his wife again. Instead, he found himself building his life over again, gaining his freedom but losing his wife.

Robert Preston Taylor had two options when he returned home: He could allow all that had happened to him to overtake him, or he could overcome. He triumphed, showing that he had the courage to not only survive, but to move on with the Lord to whatever was next in his life.

Taylor spent the rest of his career working as an air force chaplain. He married a nurse he had met briefly in the Philippines and met again in the United States. On August 16, 1962, Brigadier General Robert Preston Taylor was named Air Force Chief of Chaplains by President John F. Kennedy. Taylor served as an overseer of the leadership of all the air force clergy and was able to do great things for the Lord in his position.

Taylor knew the Lord was always with him. He knew it in his early days of ministry, he learned what it meant in those horrific years of imprisonment, and then he spent his life teaching others how to live in that knowledge. He was a man of great commitment, unwavering faith, and the deep assurance of someone who has been tested and strengthened in the Lord.